You
Will
Never be
the Same

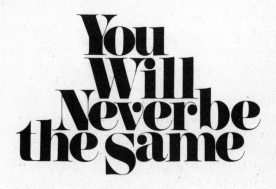

You Will Never be the Same

Basilea Schlink

BETHANY HOUSE PUBLISHERS
MINNEAPOLIS, MINNESOTA 55438

Published by Bethany House Publishers
A Ministry of Bethany Fellowship International
11400 Hampshire Avenue South
Bloomington, Minnesota 55438
www.bethanyhouse.com

Printed in the United States of America by
Bethany Press International
Bloomington, Minnesota 55438

ISBN 0-87123-661-3

Contents

PART ONE

The Wages of Sin and the Battle of Faith

1. A Conversation and its Consequences

This book has a little story behind it. Many years ago, around Christmas time, I was sitting with my spiritual daughters and we were sharing our experiences together. One of the Sisters had a request, and others joined her: "Mother Basilea, can't you tell us how to get rid of our own special sins, those obstinate ones that just seem to cling to us?"

My answer turned into a lengthy conversation, for one after another they named their sins and were eager to hear how they could experience Jesus' redemption. No one felt embarrassed in front of the others for God's Spirit of Truth was among us. Each Sister knew that she was "sick" and that she needed to be healed by Jesus. Therefore they yearned for the right diagnosis and for the right therapy.

The conversation finally ended with the request, "Please write something about the battle of faith against our sin – something that can help us in a practical way!" So I wrote a few pages about some of the sins for those who needed them and they tried out the prescriptions. After a while my daughters said that this helped them so much that it ought to be made available to all who are looking for the way out from the anguish that sin causes. So the few pages were supplemented and later published as a book. We did this with the victorious joy in our hearts: "So if the Son makes you free, you will be free indeed" (John 8:36).

The fifth German edition of this book is now being published in a revised and expanded form. The methods described have proved themselves—not only for me and many of my daughters, but also for many who have come to Canaan or who read this book elsewhere. Our retreat Sisters tell us that the meeting where they distribute the "spiritual medicine" is one of the most joyful meetings. Perhaps there is also "joy in heaven" on such afternoons when people crowd around the "spiritual drugstore" to get advice and help for their particular sins through one of the chapters of this book. It is a wonderful sight to see married couples help each other choose their medicine or see parents choose it for their children or vice versa.

When the leader of a Sisterhood abroad discovered this book and heard the testimonies of our Sisters who lived with it, she was overjoyed to receive the whole "drugstore" for all her spiritual daughters and felt that this would bring a great renewal. And why should this renewal not come about? We have found that when we really fight the battle of faith, daily trusting in Jesus and His salvation, release and transformation will really take place. To Him be thanks and adoration.

A small hint from experience; this book is not meant to be read in one sitting. The chapters about the specific sins are designed rather to help us when we go through certain periods that make us more aware of those particular sinful traits in our character. Thus the book will help us take the best advantage of such situations, as it shows us how to pray and fight a concrete battle of faith.

2. My most Important Discovery after my College Years

We are all the same. We live with our families or we spend time with other people at work or at school, and always notice their behaviour very accurately. Some are irritable and touchy; others easily lose their temper. Some are hurt so easily; others are dishonest, and still others give in to all their impulses. We find it hard to put up with these things. We are irritated every time we see people do these things. Usually we cannot say anything, because they would take it the wrong way. But if only there were a way, we would do everything we could to get rid of the blemishes in their personalities.

But there is something very strange. If we ourselves are often irritated, angry, bitter, jealous, untruthful, impulsive, we usually do not get at all excited and do not take offence at ourselves. Perhaps just because of the fact that we believe in Jesus Christ, we are convinced that we have the assurance of salvation; we are in the "boat" that will lead to heavenly glory. But we do not sense how Satan is perhaps scornfully laughing at us—and justifiably so. Without our knowing it, he has taken our boat into his hands, because we are persisting in sin.

WAKING UP

But one day I woke up spiritually. Before that I was accustomed to reacting angrily when anything did not suit me or when someone said something that irritated me. But I did not think I had done anything wrong. These reactions were beginning to become part of my personality. I had been converted, and, after all, that was the important thing. Until one day, a few decades ago, my eyes were opened. I can still remember where I was sitting when I began to cry bitterly, after I had once again "let loose" at someone in an irritated tone of voice.

What was it that made me cry? Suddenly I was faced with the fact that Jesus had paid the price of redemption for me so that I could be redeemed. Jesus had shed His blood for me so that I could be remade into the image of the Son of God. Where were the similarities between me and Jesus, the Lamb? He was meek and He had promised the kingdom of heaven to the meek. But had I become meek? My relationship to Jesus had become like a relationship to a dead person. It was almost as though Jesus had become just a mathematical formula for me. Certainly I believed that He had paid the price of redemption for me, that I had been bought free, that I was justified. But during the course of time this faith had become an empty formula.

Where was this wonderful, living Christ in my life? Because He is alive today, we can still grieve Him as much as His disciples did long ago. Yet He is the Lord whom we should not grieve, because He has laid down His life in love for us.

Now I could see how much we grieve Him and put Him to shame through our lives, when we do not fulfil His last plea, "By this all men will know that you are my disciples, if you have love for one another" (John 13: 35). That went deep into my heart: My behaviour towards my neighbour was not an example of love, but sometimes just the opposite. Love does good things for others, but I was making life difficult for others. I had taken grace for granted and accepted it lightly as if it were something cheap. Yet grace was bought for us with a high price, with the sacrificial death of Jesus, so that we can only reply to such grace by committing ourselves completely to the Lord. But then we have to hate what He hated so much and what He paid such a high price to overcome: sin. He hated it so much that He died to put an end to it.

HATRED TOWARDS SIN

Did not Jesus say, "If anyone comes to me and does not hate ... even his own life"—and by that He means our ego, our sinful self— "he cannot be my disciple" (Luke 14: 26)? I was deceiving myself! I thought I was a disciple of Jesus, but I really was not, because I did not have a hatred towards sin. At this time, more than thirty years ago, God suddenly opened my eyes and let me see what sin was all about. It has to be hated so much that Jesus says it is better to pluck out our eyes rather than give room to sin and tolerate it in ourselves. It would be better to cut off our hands than to tolerate what is evil and sinful. Now I saw that sin spreads like a cancer. But I had not recorded as sinful my rebellion and my angry reactions when I had been wronged. Suddenly I saw that it was the same in other cases. For instance, I no longer tried to do everything to "keep the Sabbath holy". And Jesus had said, "If you love me, you will keep my commandments" (John 14: 15). His commandments were, first of all, the Ten Commandments, which He interpreted with a much deeper meaning in His Sermon on the Mount, making their scope much wider. Had I not read what the disciple who was closest to Jesus had written? "He who says 'I know him' but disobeys his commandments is a liar, and the truth is not in him" (I John 2:4).

So I was a liar. And although I said I believed in Jesus, I was outside the Kingdom of God (Gal. 5: 19–21). That means that such people will be shut out from the kingdom of heaven for eternity. Jesus says the same thing with unmistakable clarity in the parable of the unmerciful servant who was bound by Satan and taken into his kingdom because he did not want to forgive (Matt. 18:32-35).

UNREDEEMED DESPITE REDEMPTION

Now I could see that there was something wrong in my life of faith. Certainly I knew about the sacrifice of Jesus. As the Lamb of God He redeemed us so that we might "walk in newness of life". But it was merely knowledge. It does not do us any good to have money in the bank, if we do not go and claim it. Nor does it do any good to know about the sacrifice and blood of Jesus, if we do not claim them. So the great grace that had been offered to me remained "dead capital". I realized then that knowledge about Jesus' sacrifice does not make us new men. Only living faith, which is put into action in a battle of faith, can do this. Holy Scripture says, "Fight the good fight of faith; take hold of eternal life" (1 Tim. 6: 12). If I am supposed to take hold of something, I have to do something myself. If I am supposed to fight, I have to make an all-out effort. And I had not made this effort. The Apostle Peter wrote—and it was directed to believers—that the "adversary, the devil, prowls around like a roaring lion, seeking some one to devour" (1 Pet. 5: 8). I had not reckoned with the truth of this fact. It means that I am in danger, even if I can show my "spiritual credentials": being baptized, converted or filled with the Spirit. I have an enemy who is always on my heels, ready to fight and get me down. He wants to have me as his prey. If the enemy is not only threatening me but has already begun to fight, I will be lost unless I take hold of weapons myself and enter the battlefield. So it is not left to our fancy whether we would like to fight the battle of faith or not, but it is a matter of absolute necessity. Otherwise we are irretrievably lost. We cannot afford to be passive and not do anything, unless, of course, we are not interested in whether we become the enemy's prey.

In the face of these facts I now realized that I had been building castles in the sky, because I had not taken seriously what Jesus and the apostles said so clearly in the Holy Scriptures. So it was no wonder that there was no victory in my life. The Holy Scriptures are permeated with the call to fight against sin so that we can overcome and attain the victory wreath. In the Book of Revelation Jesus says to the churches, "He that overcometh shall inherit all things" (Rev. 21: 7 A.V.).

THE REASON FOR JOYLESSNESS

That is why it was not surprising that, at that time, I did not rejoice over the wonder of redemption, and that others could not see the joy of Jesus in me. And it was no wonder that I was not happy. I had taken the wrong path, the path of cheap grace, which was not the way of Jesus Christ and which could never lead me to the goal. If we do not fight, we will not be crowned. And what a fight the Lord demands of us! It is a fight to the point of shedding blood, as the letter to the Hebrews tells us (chapter 12: 4).

However, I had not taken action against my particular sinful bondages every day with prayers of faith. I had not fought against my sinful traits which put Jesus to shame, and which bind me to this earth and to Satan. I had not taken seriously Jesus' command to pluck out our eyes. In other words, I should have taken up an uncompromising fight against the causes of sins. I should have had such a hatred towards everything which gives room to the evil in us that I would not rest until it had been put to death. Now, all of a sudden, I realized how unnatural my passivity was. The moment a person discovers that he has a cancer, he leaves his job and his family, undergoes an operation and probably even spends a great deal of money for it. Although such a cancerous growth can only bring him physical death, he still makes every effort to recover.

SIN IS A CANCER

And what a harmful breed of cancer sin is! Sin is something dreadful. Scripture tells us this, and the reality of life tells us it also. It is rampant in our lives; it makes an imprint on our faces and our behaviour and ruins our personality. It makes us guilty towards God and man. It makes us and others unhappy. Sin will lead us to a terrible place for eternity, a place which corresponds to its evil and darkness. It is the kingdom of darkness, which Jesus talks about so much, a place of horror and torment.

Yes, sin is a poison, which will bring us death, eternal death, a dreadful dying. That is why Jesus says to His disciples, "Do not fear those who kill the body but cannot kill the soul; rather fear him who can destroy both soul and body in hell" (Matt. 10: 28). This fear had not gone deep down in my heart. I knew this truth, but it did not radically change my life.

Actually I had the opposite attitude in my heart. I took my physical illness much more seriously than my spiritual illnesses of sin, which could really be deadly. Against the latter I had not waged a vigorous campaign to become free and healed. I did not let the knife cut into me by bringing my sin into the light and confessing it as the Holy Scriptures say we should do; "Confess your sins to one another" (Jas. 5: 16). There were several things I did not confess, because it would have cost me something—it would have injured my pride. I did not make a break with my sin. For instance, when I had a false attachment to another person, I did not endeavour to avoid her. And yet, if I were physically ill, I would take it for granted that I should go to the hospital and break away from my loved ones. Or, similarly, when I was at odds with someone, I did not go and reconcile myself with him, because it would have cost my pride too much.

SYMPATHY WITH SIN

Although I knew so much about the Bible, I had not comprehended that everything in the Bible was concerned with one thing: hatred of sin. Only for that reason does Christ's redemption have such a great significance. For as long as I let sin continue to live in darkness and did not bring it to light through confession, I tolerated it and nourished it, so that it could spread. And Satan, the lord of darkness, then had a claim upon me.

So instead of taking a stand in hatred against sin, I had words of self-pity and excuses for my sin. I felt sorry for myself, because people were making life so difficult for me. I tried to excuse my bitterness. I did not notice that this attitude let my sin grow strong and take deep roots. My motto should have been, "Death to my sin! Into the light!" But instead I handled it tenderly with kid gloves so that it continued to live.

Where did I stand at the time, even though I confessed Jesus as my Redeemer? I thought that I belonged to Him.

Yet I had more or less lost Him, because I did not keep His commandments and so I could not inherit the Kingdom of God. I was far away from Him.

SAVED — FOR GOOD?

Can we ever be sure we are saved? Yes, we can, but not with the prerequisite of cheap grace. That became clear to me. Every sinner, no matter how bad he is, can have assurance of salvation.

But he has to admit concretely the truth that he is a sinner. He has to have contrition, i.e. grief about his sins. If I am as grieved over my illness of sin as I would be over a cancer, I cannot tolerate what causes me so much pain. Then I will do everything to get rid of this pain and the sin that makes me so unhappy. And this is possible. Jesus' blood has been shed. His sacrifice at Calvary has taken place, and I can claim it. He declared, "It is finished!" And I can hold Him to it. He has given me everything; I just have to accept it. I do not have to accomplish it; He has done everything. He has already redeemed me—but I have to claim His victory.

The fact that I am a sinner and will remain a sinner all my life, cannot infringe upon my assurance of salvation. On the contrary, my assurance of salvation will be kept from becoming an empty formula of faith, if I fully realize this truth. The joyful knowledge of His forgiveness and the assurance of my salvation will always be kept fresh in my heart.

In that way I can really lie at the foot of the cross with a contrite heart and ask for grace. Then, just like the thief on the cross, paradise will be open for me. But during the last few years, before this turning-point, I had ceased to do this. I no longer cried about my sin; I had no longer had a contrite heart. So I was no longer dependent upon grace. That is why I was not filled with thanksgiving and praise for grace. For I had been living from cheap grace, which did not bring me the fruit of redemption, and the great joy of being able to reflect more and more of Jesus Himself.

It became abundantly clear that remaining in our hereditary sins and unbroken nature, without regretting it, will lead to terrible consequences. Nietzsche could defend himself by saying: "Christians will have to look more redeemed, if I am supposed to believe in a Redeemer." Countless other people who have renounced Jesus and risen up against Him, have followed Nietzsche's example, defending themselves by citing the fact that we Christians are so unredeemed. On this day my eyes were opened and I could see how wrong my attitude towards sin was. All the biblical truths not only faced me, they sank deep down into my heart and hit my conscience. Full of grief I realized what I had done by taking my guilt towards God and man so lightly. I began to hate sin, which cost Jesus so much. It is something so dreadful that it destroys both the life of the individual and of family or community. Yes, it even binds us to Satan.

LIFE'S CONFESSION — LIFE'S TURNING–POINT

This day brought me the gracious turning-point in my life. I brought my sin more radically into the light than ever before. For I could clearly see that as long as it remained in the dark, hidden from human eyes and ultimately also from my own because I did not want to confront it, it could continue to spread. I brought it into the light, because I knew that light unmasks the enemy. To bring something into the light means to confess it before God and man. So I went to someone and told him what my sin was. I called it by name. I brought it to Jesus again, in the presence of my confessor and renounced it. I knew that without this confession I would not be free; the enemy would continue to hold me in his hand with this hidden sin.

Now that sin had taken on its true meaning for me, I realized that it is not my sin itself that is the important thing, but rather my attitude towards my sin. If I keep it to myself, in my heart, either out of indifference or out of discouragement, I give Satan the opportunity and the right to use my sinning and to turn it into a fruit of hell.

But if I bring my sin to Jesus, if I confess it before men, I will find that it is blotted out in Jesus' blood. If I claim the sacrifice of Jesus again and again in the prayer of faith, I will find that "where sin increased, grace abounded all the more" (Rom. 5: 20).

THE NEXT STEP

However, confession and taking a stand against sin was not all that I had to do. Now I had to go to the particular individuals whom I had wronged, whether it was through word or deed. Although I can never actually "make amends", out of thanksgiving for Jesus' forgiveness and out of grief over what I had done to others, I was compelled to do whatever I could to heal the wounds that I had given them.

The sinful deed was now blotted out through the blood of the Lamb. I no longer needed to be despondent about it; I no longer needed to accuse myself and I no longer needed to wallow in this sin. But even though I truly believed that the sinful act—whether it was in word or deed—was blotted out through the blood of the Lamb, I also knew that the root of this sin, that is, the sinful trait, was still in me. I could sense this. And I knew that I now had to fight battles of faith proclaiming the victory of Jesus over my sin. For the blood of the Lamb has power not only to cover sin, but to free me and cleanse me from this sinful trait that lies so deep in my personality and disposition.

DAILY BATTLE OF FAITH

It is a matter of fighting an intensive and persevering battle. So I began to fight this battle of faith and I did this daily. Daily I brought my sins to Jesus and called them by name. Every day I took at least fifteen minutes to call upon His name and to pray a litany of victory such as:

"In the name of Jesus and in His wounds is victory.
    Jesus has trodden the head of the serpent under His feet.

Hallelujah! Amen.
I am free from . . ."

Each time I filled in the name of one of my sins.

I sang verses of victory:

> Let praises ring aloud this day,
> That Jesus' name has pow'r to break apart
> The fearful chains of sin that bind us*

And I praised His precious blood, because I knew that
something would then happen. To speak in metaphors,
the blood of the Lamb is the best medicine for my sinful
ailments. I cannot afford to leave it untouched. When we
praise the blood of Jesus, Satan yields. He and his demons
are standing behind the specific sins in our lives. It had
now become a great gift of grace for me to be able to
believe in Jesus, the Victor, in His sacrifice and His words:
"It is finished!", to believe in the transforming power of
His blood. If we claim this victory in faith, by glorifying
His sacrifice and His blood shed for us, we will be transformed.

> Your precious blood has such great might,
> It saves from Satan's hold so tight.
> I praise Your blood that sets me free
> From Satan's grip and tyranny.
>
> W.J. 184

Then I experienced in truth how the Lord freed me from
various sinful bondages during the course of years according to His Word, "So if the Son makes you free, you
will be free indeed" (John 8: 36). I found out that these
are not empty words. Through such a battle of faith we
can really be released from our chains. Jesus calls Himself
the Redeemer. So He cannot help but free us from our
chains of sin. His name is Yea and Amen and he will act
according to His name. It is His ministry to redeem us.

* This song along with others in this book is taken from Mother
Basilea's song book, *Well-spring of Joy.*

This knowledge filled me with great joy. There is no sin for which His redemptive power is not effective. Whether we are untruthful time and again, give in to our desires over and over again—or to envy, to being hurt, to strife, etc.—no matter what the sinful bondage is, we can be freed from it, even though we remain weak, sinful people as long as we are here on earth.

Yes, because the Victor over all sins and powers of the enemy is fighting on our side, the final victory will definitely be ours no matter how long the battle may last. There may be a long series of lost battles, but there will never be a lost war, so long as we endure in faith and do not shy away from being humiliated when we realize how tightly we are bound.

CRISES OF FAITH

Certainly it often happens when we begin to take up the battle of faith against certain sins, that everything seems to be worse than before. But then it is a matter of continuing to fight in the knowledge that the enemy is only raging and making every effort to keep his hold on us, because he knows that a mighty victory, a release, is coming. Whoever does not shy away from this fight but patiently treads the long path of humiliations will experience the redemptive power of the Victor, Jesus Christ. That I can bear witness to.

Knowing about the unconditional victory of Jesus during such times when I was in an especially difficult battle brought great joy into my heart. I have a Lord, who has sacrificed His life for me. I have a Lord who is Victor. I can fight against my sins by proclaiming, "Jesus is Victor!" I have a Lord, who, as the Lamb of God, has triumphantly broken the power of Satan and sin. This I can grasp in faith. This is the truth. And this truth will make every power of Satan and sin capitulate.

Although this book is about our various "sinful illnesses", I am writing it with great joy, because we do not have to *keep* our "sinful illnesses". When we are physically ill, we do not know whether we will get well, whether there is really a medicine that will cure us. But what a triumphant fact: we know that we can and will recover from these serious illnesses of ours, whose consequences reach into eternity, for there is a medicine which will make us completely whole. It is the blood of the Lamb, which freely flows from His wounds. Therein lies the victory. There are His words, "It is finished". There is the sacrifice on Calvary. Whoever claims these truths in fighting the battle of faith will get well spiritually. He will overcome his sins, if he is also willing to let the Lord chasten him so that "we may share his holiness" (Heb. 12: 10), and may, to Jesus' glory, reflect His image.

3. Sin: An Old-Fashioned Concept or our Worst Enemy?

Before I go into the specific sins, let me say a word about the world-wide significance of fighting our personal battle of faith against sin.

We are living in a period when sin is no longer given any meaning. It has become unimportant; it no longer counts. Today the existence of sin and Satan is being negated. The concept of "sin" has been thrown out of modern man's vocabulary, because people say that sin does not exist at all. That is why they do not have to fight against it, but rather can give it room so that it can flourish. But the reality of our times is proof that Satan does exist, that sin is a satanic power and that the results of sin are misfortune and destruction. In criminality, the increasing suicide rate and drug addiction, we can see this reality and its disastrous consequences wherever we look.

God is giving us today more visual instruction in the dreadful effects of sin than ever before. Today there is hardly anything else that we can turn our attention to other than sin. In our age it is especially true that the misfortune, destruction, criminality and decay of morality will only be hindered, if we hate sin and break with it. Above all we Christians have to take sin more seriously than ever before. For sin provokes judgment. And His Word tells us that judgment begins with the household of God (I Pet. 4: 17), that is, with us.

We Christians of today will be held especially responsible for our attitude towards sin, and will be judged according to much more severe standards, because we have received more, namely the clear directives of the will of God and at the same time the redemption from all our sins through our Lord Jesus Christ. Whenever we do not bring our sins to the cross of Jesus, confess them and turn away from them, they begin to work in our

21

personal lives. We lose peace and joy, because our sin separates us from God. But even worse, our sin brings us a terrible harvest for all eternity. We will have to suffer for it, because it will be judged very severely in the next world. The Apostle Paul tells us that even Christians must "appear before the judgment seat of Christ so that each one may receive good or evil, according to what he has done in the body" (2 Cor. 5: 10).

The sensible ones today are those who measure their sins according to the Holy Scriptures and fight a battle of faith against them in their personal lives. Whoever does this also has to take a stand against false brotherly love, which often tolerates sin. People see the main cause for all social ills and needs (for instance, slums, prisons, homosexuals and drug addicts) in the social and political conditions, in the "structure of society". And they try to do something about them through "social activism". The facts, however, prove that it is not the social conditions that are at fault for the spreading of sin. We see that the increase of crime, all the misery of the personality and of the life of a nation, is found most in socially well-off countries like the United States, West Germany and Britain. Such an avalanche of addiction and criminality, which leads to misery and corruption, can only be caused by sin. And sin is spreading, because people do not want to confront it, let alone punish it. Instead they give it free reign.

But whenever we make other people's sins seem harmless through false brotherly love, whenever we support this attitude, the reason is ultimately that we do not want to fight against our own sin, and to break with it. That means that we have gone over to the enemy's camp. For sin and Satan belong together. Jesus, who loves sinners so much, hates sin, because it is the ruin of the sinner. He has condemned it by taking it upon Himself for us, and showing us by His death that whoever sins actually deserves death.

Jesus demands that we proceed categorically against sin. "Pluck out your eye!" Do not grant it any right to live, for, "it is better that you lose one of your members than that your whole body be thrown into hell" (Matt. 5: 29). Time and again He tells us unmistakably that sin will be judged by God and that the unforgiven sin of the individual or nation will bring them misfortune here on earth and deliver them into the kingdom of darkness and horror after death. And this kingdom of hell which Jesus always talks about is a reality.

Jesus' message was "Repent!" Turn away from your sinful ways! Jesus takes sin so seriously that He not only says that the Ten Commandments are completely binding for us, but He also deepens their meaning by attacking even lustful glances and angry words. He threatened punishment in hell, if we do not regret them and repent. For God had already said that the Ten Commandments would bring disaster, destruction and severe judgment to everyone who did not fulfil them.

How seriously the apostles took sin can be seen in the New Testament epistles. They called it by name. The Apostle Paul could not only sing songs of praises for the forgiving and enduring love in 1 Corinthians 13, he could also quite soberly and earnestly demand that sinners be punished (1 Cor. 5: 5). He wrote to Timothy, "As for those who persist in sin, rebuke them in the presence of all so that the rest may stand in fear" (I Tim. 5: 20).

Whoever does not want to become guilty, by going along with sin—perhaps due to a mistaken concept of brotherly love—has to take a stand against sin. For whoever really believes in Jesus Christ and loves Him has to hate what Jesus hates, and Jesus hates sin. He cannot make sin seem to be harmless or tolerate it or no longer call crime, addiction and moral depravity sin. According to the Holy Scriptures sin is to be punished, because it brings about dreadful things, because it makes us guilty and is the ruin of ourselves and our nation.

If we Christians no longer take sin seriously, due to a misinterpretation of brotherly love, but rather seek to make it harmless and tolerate it, and perhaps even try to glorify it, like the representatives of the "new morality", we will pull others into sin also and cause them to stumble. Then we are struck by Jesus' severe verdict,

"Whoever causes one of these little ones who believe in me (the young in faith) to sin, it would be better for him to have a great millstone fastened round his neck and to be drowned in the depth of the sea" (Matt. 18:6). Yes, such false "toleration" lets sin flourish. It deprives the individual of the opportunity to experience Jesus' forgiveness through repentance and sorrow about sin. It deprives him of a genuine healing of his spiritual needs through his Saviour.

That is why our love for our neighbour is only genuine, if it is rooted in love for God. Scripture says, "By this we know that we love the children of God (brotherly love in the true sense of the term), when we love God" (1 John 5: 2). And the proof that we love God is that we "obey his commandments" (1 John 5: 2). But whoever obeys His commandments takes a stand against sin, which is from the devil. "He who commits sin is of the devil" (1 John 3: 8). It is our task to fight against Satan and sin so that lawlessness and destruction may not spread among us through our own fault, for "sin is lawlessness" (1 John 3: 4b).

The following pages seek to help us fight the proper battle of faith by drawing our attention to places in Scripture which show how God the Lord condemns the various sins and what He has to say about the dreadful effects and punishments—even to the point of hell—if we persist in them.

Because God is Yea and Amen, and because everything has always happened as He said it would, this will also come to pass. "God is not mocked" (Galatians 6: 7). What man sows through his sin he will harvest. That will determine where we spend eternity. And it is unforeseeable how many people we will pull along with us—either into eternal damnation or, because we have fought the good fight of faith, into eternal glory.

When we read such truths in the Word of God, and are confronted by them, we are tempted to join His disciples in saying, "This is a hard saying; who can listen to it?" (John 6: 60). But then we have to listen to what Jesus answered them. "Jesus, knowing in himself that his disciples murmured at it, said to them; 'Do you take offence at this? It is the spirit that gives life, the flesh is of no avail; the words that I have spoken to you are spirit and life'." (John 6: 61,63).

Because Jesus' words are spirit and life, they are not hard. If we believe them, they will free us and make us happy. Is there any grace more amazing than the offer of complete redemption by someone who is by nature a *Redeemer*, in spite of our guilt-laden past, in spite of massive bondages to sin, in spite of the hardness of our hearts, in spite of our inveterate, hereditary disposition? Did not Jesus Himself say, "So, if the Son makes you free, you will be free indeed!" (John 8: 36)?

Because God is Yea and Amen, it is true that if we take His words about sin seriously and open ourselves to judgment here, we will experience the power of His redemption and the reality of His release, which will save us from eternal punishment.

Could there be any price too high to pay for His redemption in us during this short life? After all, the affliction is but slight and momentary (2 Cor. 4: 17). Will it not be followed by an eternity where we are even to be crowned as overcomers for this short battle of faith? A wise man once said that our earthly life in comparison with eternity is like the flight of a bird through a room. It flies in one window and out the next. Its real life is spent outside. And so our time on earth is but a passing moment in comparison with eternity. And why should we spend this moment trying to spare ourselves and not fight? Yet Satan suggests that we do this. For the moment of this life he offers us permission to persist undisturbed in our sin. He uses all possible methods to soothe our consciences, by trying to get us to consider ourselves saved through "cheap grace". However, we will be shocked when our eyes are opened in the other world to see how far away we are from Jesus.

Let us not belong to those who reject as a "hard saying" Jesus' precious offer to redeem us from all our sins and let us not murmur against His conditions. Knowing that some had this attitude, Jesus said: "There are some of you that do not believe" (John 6: 64). Jesus has stretched out His hand to us and offered us eternal redemption. Who would not take His hand and be willing to pay any price to reach the highest goal that Jesus wants us to reach: the Marriage Supper of the Lamb!

4. So We are not a New Creation after all?

"If any one is in Christ, he is a new creation; the old has passed away, behold, the new has come" (2 Cor. 5: 17). Is that really true? Is the "new man", whom the Apostle Paul talks about so much, a reality or not? Jesus has actually promised this newness to everyone. But are we not usually disappointed when we look at ourselves and see just the opposite? How are we to understand this contrast? The Word of God tells us the "new creation" is a fact, but the reality which we daily experience tells us something quite different.

The solution to this problem was revealed to me after several disappointments in myself, after times of despondency and discouragement, through a deeper understanding of Scripture. For Scripture takes this contrast into account, and it also shows us the way to overcome. When the wonder of wonders has happened to us—born anew by the Holy Spirit (John 3: 3, 5)—we should sing songs of praise. For then indeed a "new man" has been born by the Holy Spirit, a spiritual man, like a new-born child. And this new man, this wonderful creation of God, proves to be alive. He has a heart that feels with God, that rejoices over the redemption of Jesus, while the natural man is indifferent and self-centred. The spiritual man in us has new eyes, new ears. He sees and perceives what he has never before noticed. He recognizes God's plan of salvation and His love in his own personal life and in the events of the times. He recognizes sin as sin and responds to Jesus with sacrificial love. He has a new mouth which pours forth words of prayer and praise.

But the birth of the spiritual man in us is not the end. When we are born anew, the spiritual man is like a small, new-born baby. And above all, the old man, the natural man, has not yet died. He has been condemned to death; he has been dethroned. And he senses this, just as Herod sensed intuitively that the Child was a threat to him and that his power would reach an end. That is why he hated the Child and sought to kill Him. And with the new birth a battle begins within us also—between spirit and flesh, between the new and the old man. "The desires of the flesh are against the Spirit, and the desires of the Spirit are against the flesh; for these are opposed to each other" (Gal. 5: 17). We must be prepared for this battle. The Holy Scriptures take this to be a reality in the life of believers.

So after we are born anew, a bitter battle begins and everything depends upon who grows and who decreases. Whose side are we on? Whom do we like? Whom do we dislike? Who will be victorious? We cannot serve two masters. We have to love one and hate the other. But how can the new spiritual man reach maturity, the "stature of the fullness of Christ" (Eph. 4: 13) and be victorious? And how will the old man be starved to death?

I would like to testify to three "musts" which help bring the spiritual man in us to growth and victory. The *first* "must" is to do everything possible to put the natural man to death. The Apostle Paul says, "If by the Spirit you put to death the deeds of the body (of the natural man) you will live" (Rom. 8: 13). This will let the spiritual man live and grow. That means taking measures against yourself, against the old man, as it is written in the Letter to the Galatians, "Those who belong to Christ Jesus have crucified the flesh with its passions and desires" (Gal. 5: 24). Therefore we have to undertake something ourselves. As Scripture says, we have to put to death the strong desires of the old man within us.

For example, the spiritual man needs a prayer life for growth. But if the natural man is ruled by an exceedingly strong need for sleep or talkativeness and does not want to give these things up, the spiritual man cannot grow. Then we cannot find time to be with Jesus, to listen to Him and to speak with Him. And if food plays too great a role, the growth of the spiritual man will also be hindered. Of course, everyone who panders to his lusts will put the spiritual man to death. But the growth of the spiritual man will also be hindered, indeed our spiritual life will finally die away, if we let the natural man live in bitterness, irreconciliation or even hatred.

If we earnestly desire the growth of the "new man", we have to be resolute in putting "to death the deeds of the body". We have to give the death blow to our lusts and other cravings by radically renouncing them. That means that we have to make an "about face", if, for example, we continually read a great deal of unnecessary things or even indecent things that awaken our lusts and strengthen them. Or if we are tempted to sit in front of the television set, we have to say, No. It means getting rid of things that steal our time and interest, that we should be devoting to Jesus. Here is where we should begin to obey the Holy Scriptures and "crucify" whatever is favourable to our old man.

But everyone who has begun to take such measures will have found that he cannot free himself. Rather, after we have entered the fight and have declared war on the old man, we are most likely to experience how often we fall down and are defeated. But in spite of all the defeats, we have given God a sign that we are willing, that we are serious when we pray for release. And then, just when we begin to moan over our inability like the Apostle Paul (Rom. 7: 24), when we begin to suffer deeply for our weakness under chastening and under seemingly useless measures taken against our ego, we are prepared for the *second* "must" that will help us become victorious in this fight. We often take this second "must" for granted, knowing that it is part of the battle of faith against sin, yet many of us do not understand how to practise it in depth. It is laying hold of the sacrificial redemption of Jesus. We have to grasp in faith what His death on the cross means for us. "As Moses lifted up the serpent in the wilderness, so must the Son of man be lifted up. that whoever believes in him may have eternal life" (John 3:14, 15).

If we look at Jesus, the Crucified Lord, in faith, eternal divine life will flow into us. That is what Scripture says. Jesus is waiting for us to call upon Him, the Crucified

29

Lord, and say, "Your blood that was shed for the redemption of the world has power to put to death my natural man, to free me from the chains that are binding me!" Yes, we may call upon the Lamb of God and rely upon the fact that Jesus has broken the power of sin of our natural man with all its urges, desires, bitterness and bondage to earthly things, people, etc. When we look at the Crucified Lord in faith, the natural man will decrease and make room for the spiritual man to grow and become mature to the point of perfection.

But this does not mean looking at Jesus only *once* and taking one deep prayerful sigh, "Set me free!" As soon as an Israelite who had been bitten by a snake turned his glance away from the serpent that was lifted up, the poison from the bite killed him. Here it is a matter of enduring and keeping faith for life. That means that we have to be fascinated by Jesus and His victorious power so much, that we constantly have to look away from our poisoned condition and continually look towards Him, our Redeemer, and say, "You will be victorious in the end!" If the bondage is strong, the battle of faith will take years. But if we fight to the point of shedding blood, we will experience that Jesus has conquered our greatest weakness and our strongest bonds. We have to proclaim the victory of Jesus day by day. I have already mentioned that I have done this every day during a set period of prayer. I proclaimed His victory over my specific sinful bondages. When I do this I have to expect that something will really happen. Jesus has suffered too much; He has sacrificed too much for me, for each one of us, not to see something of the fruit of His redemption in us.

But even if we try to "put to death the deeds of the body" and fight the battle of faith, trusting in the redemption of Jesus, the spiritual man will still not be victorious. The Scriptures clearly speak of a *third* "must" if we want to reach the sanctification of God and let the old man be put to death and the new man come to maturity. It is God's chastening. It brings our natural desires to death. So God chastens a person, for instance, who is very much bound to another person, by letting him be disappointed in this person time and again. He seeks to free him by this means. Whoever accepts this chastening by saying, "Yes, Father," will receive help in his fight against his bondages. Or a person can be hit by a serious illness which frees him from his bondage to his work or to lust. If his soulish love is crucified, there will be a free place in his heart where the Spirit of God can pour in and love for Jesus can fill more room. Then his joy in Jesus will increase. We find that this spiritual law works every time, if we love the new man and hate the old man. Then we will praise God's chastening. It helps the natural man be put to death so that the life of the spiritual man can be developed.

As we have seen, the victory of the new man, true deliverance and change in our lives will come about, if we

(1) take measures against ourselves (Romans 8: 13; Galatians 5: 4)

(2) but above all, fight the battle of faith by looking towards Jesus and using the weapons that He has given us for this fight (Hebrews 12: 1b, 2a) and

(3) at the same time accept the chastenings God gives (Hebrews 12: 10f).

These are the prerequisites for everything that is written in the following pages. I cannot give thanks enough for all the changes that have already taken place in people—among my spiritual daughters as well—who have lived according to this advice and fought the battle of faith according to these rules.

MOTHER BASILEA

It is your constant patience in faith which will decide the struggle against sin, not occasional victories or defeats.

MOTHER MARTYRIA

5. Rules for the Battle of Faith against Sin

The battle against sin is an *absolute must*, because we are threatened by an enemy who constantly incites us to sin in order to bring us to ruin.

The battle against sin can only be fought *with Jesus' attitude* against sin: Take measures, do not spare yourself, "pluck out your eye".

The battle against sin means not only recognizing our sin, but also *investing time and energy* in prayer—and also taking the next practical step of repentance.

The battle against sin means *radically turning away from sin*—taking just the opposite path.

The battle against sin means setting *definite goals of faith*—beginning with genuine repentance, godly sorrow over our sin and a broken and contrite heart.

The battle against sin entails bringing the *sinful deed* under the blood of the Lamb—but at the same time *into the light*, confessing it to others, especially those who have been involved, or whom one has hurt.

The battle against sin means to *recognize the sinful trait* behind one's sinful deed in the light of truth and to take measures against it.

The battle against sin means never growing weary of *proclaiming the victorious name of Jesus;* it involves faith that endures until the end.

The battle against sin involves *saying "Yes" to the chastening of God*, which we need for purification and release.

The battle against sin means *counting on Him who has already won this battle*—Jesus Christ, who died and arose from the dead in order to save us from our sins and grant us newness of life in Him.

PART TWO

1. Absent-mindedness: Daydreaming

We speak of the "absent-minded professor", who never knows what is going on, who forgets everything, because he is so wrapped up in his own intellectual world. In the same way, if we are absent-minded in prayer, it means we are so wrapped up in other things—just like the professor—that they always attract our thoughts like a magnet.

Not knowing what is going on, not being in prayer and not working with God can have another reason: daydreaming. Some seek refuge in certain thoughts and others take refuge in daydreams and live in an imaginary world. Whether we are absent-minded or whether we daydream, our thoughts are not under the dominion of God. We have withheld a certain section of our lives from Him. Yet we usually do not realize that our absent-mindedness and daydreaming cause us to withdraw from Jesus and His demands on us. For whether we want to cling to something that fascinates us or whether we lose ourselves in daydreaming we are keeping Jesus from coming into our hearts and dwelling there.

That has serious consequences, for whatever is not under the dominion of God, Satan takes as his sphere of influence. How often have daydreams actually led us to take a sinful path in our life? Satan took possession of our daydreams.

Such seemingly harmless dreaming is not therefore really harmless. In addition to the fact that it can lead to concrete sins, it always separates us from Jesus and therefore deprives us of the fruit of our lives for eternity.

But that's not all. Jesus says, "If a man does not abide

in me, he is cast forth as a branch and withers, and the branches are gathered, thrown into the fire and burned." (John 15:6). Here Jesus is telling us how serious the punishment will be—we will be thrown away— that is, we will be separated from Him and His kingdom above, because we lived apart from Him here on earth.

That is why we must be set free from our absent-mindedness and daydreaming at all costs. Otherwise it will bring us the greatest sorrow in all eternity—having to live far away from Jesus as an outcast. Therefore, the first thing we must do is repent, because we have lost the "first love" (Rev. 2: 4), the love that keeps us with Jesus all day long with all our heart, with all our thoughts, in all our activities.

So, if our lives are still bound to anything but Jesus, to our egos, our wishes, people or things, we must repent. This is where our wandering thoughts during prayer come from. That is why we cannot follow a conversation with others. Other ideas captivate our thoughts and fantasy all day long. It is necessary to break away from things in order to be freed. We must break away from people and groups which are not in God's will for us, or stop reading certain books and magazines, or not read too many of them, even including Christian ones. We must also stop spending so much time talking with other people if we sense that it fascinates us and has a hold upon us. It also means doing away with certain types of work and service that are not necessary and are only done to satisfy ourselves, and to use the extra time for prayer. If Satan wants to prevent you from praying by telling you it is impossible to find time, you know the answer: Where there is a will, there is a way. The more we break with other things and have time apart with God to speak with Him, the more the absent-mindedness will disappear and Jesus will take you into His world.

Often there is another root for our daydreaming and absent-mindedness: our desire to avoid the cross. We do not want to see reality with all its problems, the reality of the darkness of the world, the reality of God's holiness and our sin. We do not want to bear the consequences of this: taking the cross upon ourselves and fighting the battle of faith against our sin. Therefore, we flee into our make-believe world with our absent-minded thoughts and daydreams. But in reality we cannot get away from the difficult things. We are actually even more at their mercy, because we are separated from Jesus. We must ask the Holy Spirit to give us light about this and a deep spirit of repentance in order to make a thorough break from this dreaming.

But then it is a matter of entering a real battle, so that all our thoughts and ideas are rooted in Jesus and we really attain the stage where we abide in Him. Again and again we must fight so that our association with Jesus will not be broken by dreaming and absent-mindedness. Otherwise our days and our work will be without fruit; they will be in vain. And in the other life we will not be in His presence.

I have found something that has helped me very much. Every evening, at the end of my prayers, and in the morning, before I begin my work, I ask the Holy Spirit to admonish me, whenever I begin to lose myself in my thoughts again. And Jesus answers my prayer. He also gives me the dread and hatred of everything that seeks to destroy my relationship and union with Him, who is alone life eternal and can make my activity full of immortal fruit.

"Work out your own salvation with fear and trembling" (Phil. 2: 12). "Fight the good fight of faith" (I Tim. 6: 12). We must call daily upon the victorious name of Jesus and proclaim its power over our inability to concentrate and our dreaming. As surely as Jesus has come as the Redeemer, He will redeem us to be disciples who abide in Him and fill our life and activity with divine life and fruit. Jesus is longing for us to be with Him, because He is yearning for our love. And a sign of true love is that we desire to be intimately united with the one we love in everything we do, say or think. If we love Jesus, we have only one wish, not to lose Him during the day, not to fall out of His love—and on the other hand to prove our love for Him by giving Him everything, even our thought-world so that it may come under His dominion.

> *Keep your heart with all vigilance;*
> *for from it flows the springs of life*
> (Prov. 4: 23).

2. Anger

Usually we are not at all dismayed—especially if we are choleric by nature—if we should happen to flare up violently when we are irritated or annoyed. For instance, if we are irritated by our disobedient children, we almost think it is natural for us to shout at them. But then we are using false standards, standards that God does not accept. God's standard is different and it is the only one that is valid. We will be judged according to it. It is the standard that Jesus gives us. In the Sermon on the Mount He speaks about being angry with our brother. He tells us what will happen, if we insult our brother or even say to him, "You fool!" (Matt. 5: 22). None of us would think that this is a serious sin. Yet Jesus pronounces a frightful judgment over such vehement behaviour. He includes angry people with murderers, and a terrible punishment will await them. And we know that anger can really kill in a figurative sense. Children, and even adults, who have been victims of a constant barrage of angry remarks often have deep scars in their souls; it is as though something there has been put to death.

God's judgment will come down in a dreadful way upon those who persist in being angry. Jesus said that those who hurl angry insults at their neighbours will find their eternal place in the fire of hell, if they do not repent of their anger (Matt. 5: 22). Jesus tells us clearly and unmistakably: Just as the meek belong to Him, the angry belong to Satan and his kingdom of darkness. Therefore, no matter what the cost, we must be freed from anger, from flaring up and being vehement.

We must not fall into Satan's traps. We know his tricks. He tries to convince us that we have to shout at people every once in a while just as Jesus did when He drove the money-changers out of the temple. But when he tries this trick, we can only say: "Get behind me, Satan, you blasphemer!" Jesus was not a sinner like us, but the Holy One of God, filled with the spirit of love, and He was only acting out of the agony of love when He saw the sacred temple being desecrated by sin. He was angry, because He wanted to save; His anger was a reaction of His love

On the other hand, we really ought to know what our heart is like. It is a den of robbers. Evil thoughts come out of it (Matt. 15: 19). It is like a cup of poison. If we think we are helping others to get straight, by shouting at them angrily, we are handing them a poisonous drink. Our good intentions are mixed with bitterness and indignation. Can there be anything good or loving behind our angry, vehement words when all this is resting in our hearts? What liars and hypocrites we are, if we pretend that we just want to help the other person get back on the right path by giving him a piece of our mind. In truth we usually just want to give vent to our annoyance and anger—and because this is Satan's poison, it cannot help others and free them. It will only make them more set in their evil ways.

Satan's poison of anger and flaring up has to be removed from our hearts and lives, if we want to be free from Satan's power. And whoever fights a battle of faith in hatred against this sin will be freed from it, for Jesus has come to destroy the works of the devil. Should He not also conquer this devilish anger in us? Did not God make Moses, who killed the Egyptian in great vehemence, more meek "than all men that were on the face of the earth" (Num. 12: 3)?

We have to make an "about-face", declare war on our anger and choose the way of Jesus. "To this you have been called ... that you should follow in his steps. ... When he was reviled, he did not revile in return; when he suffered, he did not threaten" (1 Peter 2: 21–23). In our mind let us picture Jesus, who says: "I am gentle" (Matthew 11: 29)—Jesus, the Lamb of God, filled with gentleness, patience and meekness—a picture of love that overcomes all! And to this image He has redeemed us. We should reflect this love, which wins other people, which is the opposite of anger and vehemence. It is gentleness and mildness which has great power and thaws out hard hearts like a spring wind.

This way of meekness leads us to heaven. The meek are called blessed. The way of the angry leads to hell. We can choose. If we want to follow the way of the Lamb, Jesus, "the Captain of our salvation" (Heb. 2: 10 A.V.), will proceed us and we will tread in His footsteps. That means in practice: If we are upset and annoyed about something, we should not go to the other person immediately to give vent to our anger. Wait and pray first. Perhaps instead of hitting him with a long tirade, we might just write down a few lines on paper. We must never let the sun go down upon our anger, but humble ourselves before God and if necessary also before the people against whom we were angry. God will bless such steps taken in obedience and will remould us into gentler people.

Should it not be possible for God to make us gentle and meek? Jesus has paid the ransom price and broken the power of Satan and sin so that we no longer have to serve this sin of anger. We have truly been redeemed from the futile ways inherited from our fathers (1 Pet. 1: 18). The disposition of our fathers—like vehemence and anger—which we have inherited, can no longer rule over us. This sin has been nailed to His cross and our inheritance is the new disposition, the image of God. In Christ we are a new creation, redeemed to the image of the Lamb, who was meek and humble—this we must claim in faith.

3. Avoiding the Cross: Unwillingness to Suffer

How can these things be compatible: we want to be Christians, disciples of Jesus Christ, who bore the cross for the whole world and chose to do so voluntarily, and yet we reject our own cross? Jesus says, "He who does not take his cross and follow me is not worthy of me" (Matt. 10: 38), and "Whoever does not bear his own cross and come after me, cannot be my disciple" (Luke 14: 27). One day Jesus will say to those who avoided their crosses, "I do not consider you to be My disciples!" Then the door to His kingdom will be closed.

What severe judgment will come upon us, if we refuse to carry the cross that has been laid upon us and complain about it to God and man! Our complaints are usually accusations. If we bear our suffering by saying "Yes, Father" we will come to great glory one day above, and here on earth we will be led into an intimate fellowship of love with Jesus. But if we avoid the cross, we will experience just the opposite. Here on earth we will become unhappy, because we are separated from Jesus. Only those who are His true followers, who go the way of the cross with Him, will be near Him here, and then above for all eternity.

If we want to be with Jesus and want our lives to end in the City of God, there is only one way—the way of the cross. Jesus is asking each of us personally "Will you choose My way of the cross?" He is beckoning to us in love, "Come, follow Me; take up your cross!" If we do not follow the call of Him who loves us more than anyone else, if we refuse to take up our cross and even rebel against it, we will have to hear the Lord say to us as He did to Peter, "Get behind me, Satan!" (Matt. 16: 23). For then the tempter has us in his grip. He will bring all those who do not want their crosses into the kingdom of hell. Then they will have to suffer much worse. Satan wants to use every means to deter us from going the way of the cross, because he does not want us to reach the kingdom of eternal joy. There our cross will change to joy, if we carry it for Jesus here. This is a decision which will have far-reaching consequences for all eternity.

If we want to enter Jesus' kingdom one day and inherit the crown of life, we have to follow the Apostle Paul's advice, "Take your share of suffering as a good soldier of Christ Jesus" (2 Tim. 2: 3). We should surrender ourselves to suffering, for instance, if God lays a cross upon us, if we have to suffer unjustly, if people hurt us without reason, scold us and treat us badly, it is then that we must follow in His footsteps. "When He was reviled, he did not revile in return; when he suffered, he did not threaten; but he trusted to him who judged justly" (1 Pet. 2: 23). If we want to choose the "ways in Christ" (I Cor. 4: 17), we will suffer everything; persecuted and reviled, we will bless; suffering unjustly, we will be "refuse", a doormat for all. Then we are on Jesus' side. Then He will recognize us as His disciples and want to share His glory with us above, giving us thrones and crowns. Those who have suffered with Christ and have patiently borne various types of suffering and afflictions, such as bodily hardships, disappointments, loneliness, the death of dear ones and family troubles, will inherit eternal glory with Jesus (Romans 8: 17). But if we belong to those who complain about every cross and are discouraged and even accuse God with the question, "Why me? Why do I have to suffer?" we could be destroyed by God's verdict. "But as for the cowardly ... their lot shall be in the lake that burns with fire and brimstone ..." (Rev. 21: 8).

So everything depends upon whether we really bear our crosses. But how can we get free when we are bound by fear of the cross? The first "must" is to recognize the reason for trying to avoid the cross! We need the insight of truth for our unredeemed, sinful nature. We need to repent of this sinful trait, which makes us guilty again and again. Whoever has recognized how contaminated he is with sin, and is really sorry about it and wants to be freed no matter what it costs, will willingly accept discipline and suffering of all sorts from God. For he tells himself soberly, "I need the crosses to purify and transfigure me into the image of Jesus and so reach the goal of heavenly glory." But whoever does not take his sins and the eternal goal seriously will find that every type of suffering is too much for him. He will complain about it and accuse God and man instead of honestly admitting that he needs suffering and chastening, and lamenting about his own weaknesses and sins. So we need to ask for contrition over this blindness. Then our attitude towards the cross will change and we will see His blessing in it.

Simply by suffering in the flesh we stop sinning (1 Pet. 4: 1). God allows a cross to enter a sinful area of our lives—so that the sin may be put to death, in this way we become transformed more and more into Jesus' image and one day will be able to see Him face to face. Through discipline we share His holiness (Heb. 12: 10) and without holiness, no one will see the Lord (Heb. 12: 14). For instance, the cross of losing earthly goods, if willingly accepted, has often freed people from their bondage to things of this world, making them free to live for Jesus and His kingdom. Or the cross of losing a beloved person, to whom we were bound, freed our soul to give Jesus undivided love and brought the greatest happiness into our hearts. The cross brings glory and deep joy even here on earth, because God the Father in His love cannot wait until eternity; He yearns to reward us here also.

The second "must" for becoming free from trying to avoid the cross is to look at the Father, whose heart is full of love for His child and who carefully considers how much we can bear and what will be best for us. He gives us the very cross that can bring us to glory. He hides a wonderful treasure in our cross. We are to discover it: wonderful fruit, transfiguration, victory, eternal joy, oneness with Jesus. And we must tell ourselves again and again, "Because God is love, suffering is never the end of the story. God always has a way out of suffering; He always has comfort and aid, for He is my Father." Faith in the Father's love, which has given us this cross, will make difficult things easy and bitter things sweet.

At the same time look at Jesus. He was the Cross-bearer. Humbly bending beneath the heavy burden, He carried His cross lovingly to Calvary for us. He has gone on before us and levelled the ground for us so that we will not stumble. Now He is bearing our cross with us. He knows what it means to carry the cross, since He bore the sins and suffering of all mankind. He knows how to help and strengthen us. Should we not trust Jesus that we can bear it? Yes, if we bear our cross with Jesus, we will come closer to Him than ever before and experience His joy.

So let us renounce our mistrust and stop thinking that God is not love and that He brings us suffering without comfort and aid. For such thoughts nourish our desire to avoid the cross and turn our cross into an unbearable burden. Then we will really become unhappy. The worst suffering is our own desire to avoid the cross. That is why we want to renounce this sin. In faith we want to praise the power of Jesus' redemption and experience this power in our lives.

My Lord Jesus,

You are called the Crucified Lord and the Cross-bearer. I have chosen You as my Lord, given You my will and my love, desiring to follow You.

Hear my plea:

May You never have to say to me: "You are not worthy of Me; you cannot be My disciple", because I did not want to carry my cross.

Grant me the grace to say "Yes Father" to every cross, trusting that it has been prepared for me personally and comes from the loving hands of the Father. It will bring me an abundance of divine blessing.

Grant me grace to rejoice in my sufferings (Rom. 5: 3), because they transform me and prepare me for Your kingdom of joy and glory—and also give me intimate fellowship with You, my Lord Jesus, here on earth, and let me taste eternal joy.

I thank you, my Lord Jesus, for showing us:

In the cross is great fruit
in the cross is glory
in the cross is victory, power and resurrection.
The cross frees my soul from this earth and draws me to heaven.
The cross brings me gain here and above.
Teach me to love my cross as a precious gift from Your hand, which I will thank You for in eternity. Out of love for You, my Lord Jesus, I wish to follow You. Make me a true cross-bearer. Amen.

4. Being Annoyed: Irritability

Being annoyed! Can that really be a sin? Or is it merely a slight personality flaw, which anyone could afford to have? Annoyance usually stems from being offended when people say or do things that do not suit us. Scripture tells us what this can lead to. In several places it is written that people "took offence" at Jesus (John 6:61, also Matt. 15: 12). They began with "mere" annoyance, but what terrible consequences this can have! The people of His home town also took offence. Then they led Him out of the town and tried to put Him to death by pushing Him off a cliff (Luke 4: 29). Such annoyance was the cause of great suffering for Jesus and great guilt for men. Today too, annoyance has similar effects.

So often in everyday life we see the alarming results of this seemingly harmless sin. How often is a relationship of love disturbed, because someone gets annoyed? Then we begin to wrong each other. That can happen in many different ways. For instance, many marriages have gone on the rocks, because one of the marriage partners was always annoyed whenever they had anything to discuss. Peace was disturbed. Every objective discussion was made impossible and they could no longer approach each other in love. Often, for this reason, children have lost their confidence in their parents or teachers, who were always annoyed with them. And we make our colleagues at work feel unhappy when we are continually annoyed. They no longer feel like working. By being annoyed, we can destroy things that we cannot make amends for.

Why do we get annoyed? Because we are not at one with the will of God. That is why everything that does not suit us upsets us. We object to everything. Or demands are made on us which we think are too much. Or someone's request upsets our intentions and we react with annoyance. But we do not realize that all things, large and small, that come from people, are actually

45

placed in our daily lives by God. When we get upset, we rebel against God and grieve Him. And why do we get annoyed at people, at situations and conditions? Because our ego or our self-will is so big. Everything has to go the way we intended, the way we think is right, the way that is easiest for us. Every wish, opinion or mistake that others make meets with our opposition.

This annoyance or irritation is just as dangerous and sinful as anger. Anger seems to be more uncouth. But usually it only comes over us every once in a while. People who tend to be annoyed are almost always annoyed. Indeed, they even get into the habit of talking this way. They have no idea that they have become instruments of Satan, who wants to destroy peace and the fellowship of love. Then he will reach his goal and we will be acting against the very wishes of Jesus; "By this all men will know that you are my disciples, if you have love for one another" (John 13: 35).

Scripture says; "Let no evil talk come out of your mouths, but only such as is good for edifying, as fits the occasion, that it may impart grace to those who hear" (Eph. 4: 29). That is, we should speak that which will do others good and serve to bring peace. But annoyance only brings about the opposite, and for this reason we have to become free from it. Otherwise we are a disgrace to Jesus through our words and reactions.

When we are annoyed, our faces are sullen and we reproach others. Annoyance hinders joy and ruins life together. But the Kingdom of Jesus Christ is a kingdom of joy and peace. Annoyance does not fit in. Therefore, it has to be overcome; it cannot have any more room in our lives.

We often try to make excuses for being annoyed. We say it is due to weak nerves or because we are "down". But irritation and annoyance come from our evil hearts and ultimately do not have anything to do with fatigue or weak nerves. Having weak nerves or being overworked just brings out what is really deep down in our hearts. When we get into such situations, we have no reason to excuse ourselves or even to pity ourselves. But

46

we have every reason to repent and to call upon the name of Jesus. In this way we will be set free from these evil things that come from our hearts, are expressed by our tongues and disrupt the peace.

The most important thing is to recognize that annoyance—along with many other sinful ailments that we usually do not count as sin—is really a sin. It must disappear from our lives. Once we recognize this, we will rely upon Jesus' redemption and His blood, which contains healing for every sin. Then we will bring this sin to Him. Then we will become ashamed whenever we become annoyed, because we know that we are making Jesus sad and that we are becoming guilty by destroying some of His kingdom. Then we must follow Jesus' call: "Repent!" Turn away from this path of yours, do not give annoyance any more room!

This has to happen when we become conscious of our first annoyed thought. Then we have to proceed against it immediately and counter it by saying: God has ordained this. This situation, this word, this person, or whatever it may be, was actually sent to me by God. It is part of His plan. Then annoyance loses its power. And if it should escape us in a critical situation and explode in our speech, let us ask forgiveness immediately. Hating sin and being sorry for it drive us to settle accounts with God every night and tell Him when we are annoyed. If we call upon Jesus to forgive us, we must also be ready to repent concretely, to ask people whom we have grieved for forgiveness, if we have not already done so. Practising this surrender of our wills to the will of God in everyday situations and fighting the battle of faith by praising the blood of Jesus, which always sets us free, will lead to release from this sin as well.

5. Busyness

Busyness! Do we sometimes imagine that this is something good? That energy and industriousness stand behind it? Or at least that it is necessary so that we can achieve something? No. Busyness separates us from Jesus. It is a sin and has a negative effect upon my life of faith.

Everything depends upon whether or not I am at one with Jesus. Jesus says, "He who abides in me, and I in him, he it is that bears much fruit" (John 15: 5). Only what we do in union with Jesus, who is "Life", will have divine life and never perish. Only that will we be able to find as fruit in eternity.

But we know that Satan makes every effort to rob us of this eternal fruit. He wants to hinder us, at any cost, from spending the day united with our Lord Jesus, because he knows that this oneness with Jesus makes us strong. Then we are at one with the Lord of heaven and earth, who has power over every name that is named. His power is then ours and provides blessing for our work. On the other hand, if we poor sinners are separated from Jesus, we can only do worthless things, that will blow away like chaff, no matter how good they may look at first.

That is why Satan tries every possible trick to make our work completely captivate us and thus separate us from Jesus. Work can chain us, because it interests us too much, because it satisfies our human desires and because we find our fulfilment in it. Work can incite our ambition. We want to attain many things and receive success and recognition. Some just love to work. They like to see what they can do. Or work can become an escape, a way to deaden our consciences, because we have not kept our lives straightened out. During such periods our prayer-times become quite unbearable. Some people who have a great deal to do fall into the mad rush. They are wound up and therefore cannot pray while they work.

So Satan comes at us from various directions and tries to drive us into busyness, into a life without Jesus, for Satan is the malicious spirit of unrest. Jesus, however, is the Prince of peace. Whoever does His work with Him is in peace and does not rush. Then our industrious work is not a mad rush. We are not enslaved to work and driven by it, but we work together with God, drawing our strength from our times of quiet. It is full of divine life, zeal and joy.

But even though we know that we are only unhappy when we are separated from Jesus, there are usually chains binding us to our work. Again and again we have to lament that we lose our communion with Jesus during the course of the day. Indeed, when we are engaged in our various tasks, we tend to forget Him for hours. But this busyness in our work can no longer be tolerated in our lives. It is not simply harmless "rushing" or "losing one-self in the work", rather it is a sin which will bring us the most severe punishment. Who has ever applied Jesus' words seriously to his own busyness? "If a man does not abide in me, he is cast forth as a branch and withers; and the branches are gathered, thrown into the fire and burned" (John 15: 6) "Cast forth" is the fate of the busy. They will be cast forth from the countenance of Jesus and His kingdom, because they did not work for God in personal love for Him and in His sight. Not only will his works be burned, but also he himself. So we must be redeemed from busyness, no matter what the cost.

But how do we get there? "Abiding in Him", doing everything together with Jesus, is a matter of practice. We should practise saying the name JESUS over and over again in our heart. While we are working, we should practise saying, "For You! For You!" Before going to sleep, let us ask ourselves whether we were with Jesus during the day. Let us ask the Spirit of God to admonish us the next day to think about Jesus. During our morning prayer before work, let us lay this request before Him again. And if we suffer especially under the sin of busyness, we should let Him show us how we can be reminded at work to speak a prayer every hour.

We must not stop beseeching the Lord for this "abiding in Christ", even if we experience many defeats. Every time we have lost the inner contact with Him at work, we should try to tie the bond anew, though it may be a hundred times a day. The fruit of our work for all eternity depends upon this. We must set for ourselves a definite goal of faith. And let us ask Jesus every day:

> Let me be immersed in You, deeper and deeper, until I can no longer lose You. Set me free through the power of Your blood from my bondage to work!

God will answer and we will experience that Jesus *is* a Redeemer, who will set us free from the chains which bind us to our work. Then we will be bound to Him and bring forth eternal fruit to His glory.

> Jesus, You are my everything!
> I will talk with You and work for You!
> I want to plan, consider and make all my decisions with You!
> Nothing shall be done without You, lest You should become an outcast.
> Bind me tightly to You, so that nothing can separate us during the day: no work, no burden, no other interest, no joy.
> May I evermore live in Your holy presence,
> For You are here!

6. Conceit: Vanity

A conceited person! These words are not exactly what you would call a compliment! Yet the highest goal of a conceited person is to be complimented. Externally he tries to have an attractive appearance and wear smart clothes. Internally he seeks the façade of a pleasant personality. His basic motive is to make a good appearance in public, to attain respect and affection. The conceited person is strongly attracted to the mirror. He looks at himself and enjoys what he sees. In a figurative sense he also looks at all his reactions, activities and conversations in a mirror and takes pleasure in them.

The vain and conceited forget, however, that there is another mirror—the eye of God, which shows us the truth about ourselves, what is behind the façade. Then we see how "vain" everything really is, how transient and perishable. But if we avoid the mirror of God, we are deceiving ourselves with the mirror of human eyes which we look into all the time with the questions: How do others react to us? Are we good-looking? Are we popular? Then our conceit grows and grows, but in the end it will make us unhappy. For the greater it becomes, the more it begins to tyrannize us. We can no longer do anything without reflecting on how others will react. We make others around us feel uneasy, because at least unconsciously they feel the demands of our ego, our vanity.

Vanity places the ego on the throne. It idolizes the ego and that is why it is a great sin. Every idol takes over the place that God ought to have in our life. That is why the same verdict that God pronounced over the idol-worshippers will hit us. For we cannot serve God and our ego-idol. We want others to burn incense to our ego. Our conceitedness wants others to admire our looks, our intelligence, our talents and our abilities and burn incense to them. In some cases this is combined with addiction to worldly riches. Then we spend great sums of money for an expensive wardrobe and other things that might help us gain the admiration of others.

But above all, conceit, the desire to be pleasing to our fellow-men, makes us insensitive to the most important thing for our life here and in eternity: that we be pleasing to God. No one will be pleasing to God by presenting an attractive appearance or displaying his talents and abilities. Only those who do not want to be anything in the eyes of men will attain God's good pleasure. This is the point we have to come to. It would be terrible to lose the pleasure of God while seeking pleasure from men. Then we will be far away from Jesus. That is why we have to repent completely.

The first step to getting rid of this sin is to admit honestly that we are vain and conceited. If we let the light of God show us this, we can only say; "How could I ever be conceited? My sins are so ugly. Even if I should be especially attractive or gifted, what does this matter in the eyes of God, who knows what really is in my heart? I ought to be ashamed of being so far away from God, because I am pleased with my poor and ugly being."

Now we must ask for "eye salve" (Rev. 3: 18). What does that mean? It means that we ask God and other people to tell us what we really are like without sparing our feelings. That will hurt, but it will help us to see the truth about ourselves. We must also ask the Lord; "Prevent me from hearing anyone praise me, and bring as much of my sin as possible into the light, so that I can see it more clearly. Then I will have to be ashamed and will lose my conceit. Yes, I even ought to tell others what I really am so that I will be humbled and learn not to live from their favour, but from the forgiveness and mercy of God."

Another step to becoming free from vanity is to reveal our conceited thoughts, to confess them to another person. If we want to receive grace from God, we have to be free from conceit and vanity, because grace is only given to the humble and contrite sinners, who are no longer pleased with themselves. But if we continue to admire our supposed qualities in the mirror and let our left hand see what our right hand has done, we have already had our reward (Matt. 6: 1 ff).

There is One who found no pleasure in Himself, and He is the only One who deserved to find pleasure in Himself: Jesus (Rom. 15: 3). And in Him we are righteous, that is, we have been set right from every sin, including vanity and conceit. That is why we should praise Him in faith, saying: "Jesus will set us free from this sin. He will remake us into His image which is free from vanity and conceit. He will change our hearts so that we will no longer seek to be pleasing to men, but only to God."

7. Cowardice

Coward! That seems to be a despicable word. A coward is someone who is afraid to show his allegiance when it costs something, who fears to confess allegiance to his social class, nation or to a certain group and its principles when they are despised, disdained or attacked. But cowardice—despicable as we think it is—exists in all of us, even if more or less hidden. A coward runs away when the enemy comes near. The disciples were cowards when they ran away, when Jesus was in danger and taken prisoner. Cowards lack courage. What kind of courage is meant here? It is the courage to suffer, to be despised and disdained, the courage to lose one's life. Cowards want to keep their lives and what makes life worth living for them, what they think is important and worthwhile. Cowards want to save their happiness, their reputation, their income, and everything they enjoy. That is why they evade the issue when their happiness, reputation or their life is threatened.

Cowardice is nothing more than a consequence of being afraid of bearing the cross. Cowardice usually goes hand in hand with fear, especially with the fear of suffering. This fear, this cowardice, often leads to short circuit reactions which could cause us to become very guilty, or could make us deny people, even Jesus and His church. Cowardice often makes us untruthful, inconsiderate and irresponsible. It can even allow others to suffer in order to save our own skin. Out of cowardice Peter denied his Lord; the disciples left Jesus in the lurch. Cowardice has caused, or at least not done anything to prevent, countless disasters.

What catastrophic consequences cowardice had for the German people during the Third Reich! And when the time of the Antichrist arrives and everyone worships his image and has to bear his mark (Rev. 13: 15, 16), the main reason for betraying Jesus at this time will be cowardice. It will have terrible consequences. These people are threatened with the punishment of God: "he shall drink the wine of God's wrath ... and he shall be tormented with fire and brimstone in the presence of the holy angels and in the presence of the Lamb. And the smoke of their torment goes up for ever and ever; and they have no rest, day or night" (Rev. 14: 10, 11). Our cowardly behaviour can bring us such judgment in eternity if we do not repent and turn over a new leaf.

That is why we have to hate this sin and begin an all-out fight against it today. Yes, if confessing the name of Jesus and upholding the commandments demands courage in our times, we absolutely must overcome our cowardice; in the future much more courage will be demanded, when people will not only ridicule the believers, but will also lay their hands upon them. If we tolerate our cowardice and make it seem harmless, we will deny and betray our Lord Jesus Christ and lose the heavenly glory for all eternity.

The important question is: How can we overcome our cowardice? One way is to dedicate ourselves to suffering. We should surrender ourselves by writing down our dedication. Furthermore we must be willing to take upon ourselves all the difficult things that we are afraid of and that may be in store for us. And we must say; "My Father, I do not know how I will be able to bear the difficult things if they should come, but I am counting on Your help. You will make me strong and pull me through. FATHER, I believe in Your love, which has already taken into account what I can bear and will not let me be tempted beyond my strength. If the difficult things should really come, I know that You, my FATHER, will comfort and refresh me in my suffering, even in martyrdom."

Yes, we must believe that we will taste heaven in the midst of suffering. And then, when we are deprived of people, things, love and honour, we will be happy, because Jesus will come to us as the Prince of Joy. In experiencing His love, our sorrow will be changed into joy, as many people who were in prison and concentration camps can testify.

Because suffering is never the end in God's plan, He will afterwards prove His goodness to us all the more. Jesus Himself trusted His Father and experienced that the Father sustained Him throughout the fear and horror of Gethsemane.

Thus we can surrender ourselves into the kind hands of God, to the loving will of the Father and take the sting out of the difficult things by saying to the Lord; "In faith, I want to go the way that You have planned for me, even if it is difficult for me. You will shed light on my dark path and make it straight for me." Then our hearts will be in peace. Fear and cowardice will be broken, because we have yielded to the difficult things which the coward always wants to escape.

The second way to overcome our cowardice—and if we neglect this, we will never be free—is to take Jesus at His word. With compassion He said, "In the world you have tribulation", but He also added, "But be of good cheer: I have overcome the world" (John 16: 33). He has trodden fear beneath His feet. And we will find, if we claim this statement, that fear will no longer be able to rule over us. His peace will come into our hearts.

Jesus has promised us, "My peace I give unto you. Let not your hearts be troubled, neither let them be afraid" (John 14: 27). And this He will do, if we expect it and call upon the victorious name of Jesus, proclaiming its power over our fear. Just as the cowardly disciples became strong after Pentecost, we too become strong men, who are not afraid of humiliation, disgrace, persecution or laying down our lives. Jesus, who powerfully changed His disciples through the Holy Spirit, is the same Lord today. He will turn us cowards into people who will testify to their convictions and be true disciples of Jesus, who are faithful to Him and will attain the crown of life (Rev. 2: 10).

8. Criticizing: Judging

Included in the sins of pride, which God treats especially severely, are the sins of criticizing and judging. "God opposes the proud" (I Pet. 5: 5). Even if a person believes in Jesus, if at the same time, he persists in judging others God is not for him. Then God has to be *against* him. But it would be terrible to have God as our opponent, to be under His wrath, which will have its full effect in the other world. That is why Jesus warns us so sharply: "Judge not, that you be not judged. For with the judgment you pronounce you will be judged" (Matt. 7: 1, 2).

Judging others will bring the wrath of God down upon us. He will be against us, because this sin is especially satanic. Judging others and accusing them is what Satan does. He is the accuser. Judging is one of the manifestations of our pride, manipulated by Satan. In great presumptuousness we sit in judgment on everything that we see or hear about others, usually without knowing the background and the motives of their behaviour or mistakes. Judging is satanic poison in our hearts, which can bring us terrible judgment, if we persist in it. Jesus tells us this clearly by addressing those who judge with the words; "You hypocrites!" (Matt. 7: 5). Jesus threatens the hypocrites, saying they will not enter His kingdom, but the kingdom of hell; they will go to the "father of lies". So the spirit of criticism, nourished by the accuser, is our greatest enemy. We have to hate it from the bottom of our hearts and not tolerate it in the slightest, unless we want to find ourselves in the kingdom of the accuser instead of with Jesus.

How can we attack this enemy? First, recognize the fact that we are full of criticism and stop trying to explain it away. We should no longer make excuses for ourselves by saying, "I have to tell others what they are doing wrong to prevent them from making a mess of things." In reality, however, we enjoy correcting others and reproaching them. Often the real source of our criticism is rebellion or annoyance, because someone did something against our wishes.

Therefore, we criticize him and accuse him. So in the light of God we have to ascertain that it is presumptuous to accuse others, to reproach them and especially to pronounce our verdicts in front of someone else. Then we will become guilty towards our neighbour, by getting others to be against him, and this could seriously harm him. When we search our conciences in our quiet time, we should ask ourselves: Where have I brought guilt upon myself by judging others and reproaching them? What has my spirit of criticism brought about? Perhaps it has even ruined people's lives. Have I harmed the souls of people at home or at work by reproaching them again and again and continually accusing them? If we— perhaps as a parent or educator—have filled our hearts with this satanic poison and sprayed it out at others, we have to admit that we are subject to God's condemnation, that we were Satan's servants.

What a terrible harvest we will reap! Our criticism will rob us of the most precious gift that Jesus has given us: forgiveness and the blotting out of our sins. Criticism provokes the wrath of God, who has forgiven us, as the parable of the unmerciful servant tells us. Although He had forgiven this servant, He delivers him to the jailers, because this servant would not forgive his fellow-servants (Matt. 18: 32–34).

So it means that we have to make every effort to get free from this spirit of criticism and whole-heartedly repent. Here we must act according to Jesus' words, "If your eye causes you to sin, pluck it out!" (Mark 9: 47). That means waging an intensive battle against the satanic sin of judging others. Jesus clearly shows us the way and we have to follow it. Otherwise there will be no release. "First take the log out of your own eye!" (Matt. 7: 5). Jesus is exhorting us: Stop giving your opinions about others and accusing them, before you become quiet in the presence of God and ask Him whether you are guilty of the same sin. Our sin of criticism usually begins when we neglect to do this. We do not follow Jesus' words; we criticize immediately without first becoming silent in the presence of God and humbling ourselves under our sin which is even greater. When we come into the light of God, we will usually find out that we have the same faults, perhaps even more dominantly and many other undesirable traits in addition. Then we will see that our guilt is like a log in contrast to our brother's splinter. We will be ashamed of our own sin and lose our presumptuous and indignant desire to criticize others.

Then we will be struck by what the Apostle Paul writes, "Therefore you have no excuse, O man, whoever you are, when you judge another; for in passing judgment upon him you condemn yourself, because you, the judge, are doing the very same things." (Rom. 2: 1). And further: "Why do you pass judgment on your brother? Or you, why do you despise your brother? For we shall all stand before the judgment seat of God"—and be judged for this sin (Rom. 14: 10).

So today we must choose a new way, a new place. Instead of sitting on the judgment throne above the others we must sit where we deserve to sit: in the defendant's box, where we can be judged and hear God's judgment on our sins. When we are willing to do this, God will no longer be against us and we will no longer be in the hand of the accuser. On the contrary, we will belong to our Lord Jesus, who had to let Himself be accused in five trials. He did this, although He was innocent. Shouldn't we, who are guilty, be able to take this place? If we earnestly begin to judge ourselves, we will ask people at home and at work to tell us the straight truth about ourselves. Humbled beneath this, we will be able to accept the reproaches of others, even when they are unjust. Then our lips and hearts will be silent and we will not be able to criticize others so quickly and judge them so harshly.

Jesus went the way of humble love. He humbled Himself in the dust and let Himself be judged. Now He has redeemed the members of His body to live this love, which covers up others' mistakes instead of criticizing, which forgives and tolerates instead of making reproaches, which bestows kindness instead of criticism.

This does not mean tolerating sin. But if we should ever have to pronounce judgment, we will do it quite clearly but with a humble and loving heart.

But whoever wages a war of life and death against his spirit of criticism will find that nothing sits so deeply in our Adam's nature as the spirit of criticism. It will not disappear overnight by making one commitment, "I want to let myself be judged and place my mouth in the dust." No, our blood is infected with it. There is only one Person who is stronger than our old Adam. It is Jesus Christ. His blood has greater power than the blood that we have inherited from our fathers. This blood of Jesus has complete power to free us, if we call upon it ever anew; in it there is really power to cleanse us from our sins, from the great sin of judging others, from hypocrisy, which makes us guilty and brings us into Satan's hands. In faith we must appropriate the redeeming power of this blood. This will only happen in an intensive fight against this sin, in a daily battle of faith and prayer. This includes speaking the "nevertheless" of faith in spite of the defeats we experience: "I am redeemed to love and to forgive!" Whoever is willing to endure in this battle in spite of his short-comings, believing in Jesus' redemption, will be freed from his great sin of judging others.

9. Curiosity

Curiosity is different from being interested in something. Being interested is something good. Curiosity is something bad. Curious people usually look at things and listen to things that are not meant for them. Typically they read letters and notes on other people's desks, that were not meant for their eyes. Or they listen to something not meant for their ears, but told confidentially to someone else. Curious people "poke their noses" into everything and make it difficult for others to live with them. They ruin community life, which is based upon trust, because they insist upon knowing everything that is going on. And they constantly seek to find out things about others. If this yearning to know things is so strong in us, there is something sinful behind it.

Curious people should ask themselves what their motives are. For instance, if they are always curious, it may be their desire for attention. Pretending to be important, they pass on their newly-gained information to others when it is not right, they talk about things in the wrong place, and they destroy the relationship of mutual confidence for the sake of being the centre of attention. If they are only curious about one person or a few people—if a mother secretly reads her daughter's diary or her children's letters about their friendships—then it probably stems from jealousy or the thirst for power. They want to pry into the secrets of others. They are hurt if they do not get to know everything and consequently they ask questions, directly or through others. They want to know everything in order to keep the other person under their control. Certainly justified concern can be one of the motives for such behaviour, but discovering things secretly is never the way to form or maintain a relationship of mutual confidence.

Sometimes mistrust is behind curiosity; or the root may be lack of discipline when confronted with sensual attractions. They are so eager to hear something new or something intimate that they overrun all ethical and moral boundaries to satisfy their curiosity. Due to this lack of discipline curious people are often driven to reading lewd literature or watching bad television programmes. If they happen to see something "by chance", they have to keep watching, just because they think they have to know what is being shown. Without their realizing it, poison can flow into their thoughts and hearts.

Because curiosity is a vice, a sin, curious people often find that God punishes them in the act. For instance, they may hear something that provokes their jealousy and then they react meanly. Or they read something that is not meant for them and do not understand the context. So they draw false conclusions, burden others unnecessarily, and spread rumours.

In all this the curious become guilty. They trespass especially against the seventh commandment. For if I have listened to or read things that do not belong to me, I have become a thief; I have stolen intellectual material, which is often much more important than material possessions. If these possessions are gained dishonestly, this can hurt others more than anything else. If someone is harmed by the curiosity of another, he sometimes finds that what he had guarded as his property is now trampled under foot by others. Curious people, therefore, are thieves, who harm others in very delicate matters, by robbing them of the possessions of their spirit and soul.

This sin is therefore against the seventh commandment. Just like every other sin against our neighbour, it will bring us God's judgment, if we persist in it. Sin always provokes God's anger, especially when it appears in Christians who know about Jesus' sacrificial death and His redemption and still dare to live in their old sins without fighting against them. If we confront this truth soberly, we will realize that we cannot continue to live with this sin. We have to begin a real battle of faith. So when we are tempted to read shameful literature or do similar things out of curiosity, we must realize that this mania can very quickly lead us into "enemy's territory", especially in our days. Then we would be like a child who goes into a forest without protection in order to see what's there and is then attacked by wild beasts.

Furthermore we must realize that it is Satan who incites us to discover new things and to know and hear what we actually should not. If we give in to our curiosity, we have fallen into his trap and he laughs at us scornfully, because he succeeded in making us sin and become guilty towards others. We must confront curiosity as a sin and not tolerate it any more in our lives. We have to be consistent in avoiding certain places, certain books and other things that our curiosity wants to drive us to. Furthermore, if we looked at or listened to something that was not meant for us, it would be advantageous for us to confess it immediately. That will make us humble and prevent us from trying to satisfy our curiosity so quickly again, because we try to avoid humiliations.

Jesus has come to redeem us from all sin, even from the sin of curiosity. Whoever calls upon Him will be saved. So we must do that and honour Jesus by not persisting in a single sin, not even in this sin which seems so small to us, because if we do, we will be disgracing Jesus, who died to free us from our sins.

10. Desire for Attention and Recognition

Two pictures are placed before our eyes. The first is Jesus wearing the crown of disgrace. Voluntarily He chose to be the most despised and unworthy One among men. People hid their faces from Him, and "we esteemed Him not". Jesus! He is the One who deserves all honour in heaven and on earth, but He sacrificed Himself out of love for us and let Himself be disgraced.

In the other picture are we men, more or less wearing sparkling crowns of our own desire for attention and respect. We are much addicted to this desire. No matter what the price is we want to be the centre of attention. We make every effort to attain this goal and all other goals become secondary. The flagrant contrast between these two pictures shows us clearly how serious this sin is. It shows that our desire for attention flatly contradicts our divine calling to be remade in the image of Jesus.

The roots of this sin lie in Adam's fall. Through the fall everything lost its proper relationship. No longer are we primarily interested in being respected by God, being at one with Him in love. Instead we have a strong drive, often a passionate yearning, to be respected and esteemed by people. If we sense that people whom we respect and whose opinion is important to us, do not respect us, we become sad, depressed, unhappy and touchy.

But that is not all. In our desire for recognition we often seek to get into the limelight and pretend to be something we are not, or to have abilities we do not possess. So we become untruthful and, without realizing it, hypocritical. We think we are serving God, but in reality we are doing everything for our own honour, so that others will respect us, and thus we sin against the most sacred things. Then the "Woe" that Jesus said to the Pharisees also applies to us. "They do all their deeds to be seen by men . . . they love the place of honour at feasts and the best seats in the synagogues, and salutations in the market places" (Matt. 23: 5–7).

These hypocrites, to whom Jesus said "Woe", are threatened by Jesus' greatest judgment in eternity. That is why we cannot tolerate the desire for recognition and attention any longer. And this desire gives rise to so many other sins.

We hurt others, we are unloving and place them in the shadow, so that we can appear in a favourable light. Especially in our times, when it will cost us increasingly more and more dishonour, ridicule and disgrace to belong to Jesus and follow Him, our desire for recognition can be our downfall and can even cause us to deny Jesus. Yes, if this addiction to receiving honour from people is so strong in us, Jesus must lament over us—as He did over the Pharisees who did not accept Him, "How can you believe, who receive glory from one another, and do not seek the glory that comes from the only God?" (John 5: 44). So this sin of desire for recognition which is usually anchored in our personalities, separates us from Jesus and the divine life. That is why we have to get rid of it no matter what the price may be. What can help us?

First of all, we have to let the Spirit of God show us again and again how despicable our desire for recognition is, and then make a definite renunciation: "Lord, I do not want to be anything; I do not want to be respected." And then we will find that there is power in this resolute renunciation. Jesus accepts it. He, the Son of God, surrendered Himself to being despised and rejected by all. Now He can help us. What is His is ours. He has gained this humility, this desire to be nothing. Then we will receive the greatest gift. We will be respected by God. The Father said that He was well-pleased with His Son when He went down into the River Jordan and let others think that He was a sinner, not worthy of respect. This "going down" brought Jesus special love from the Father and gave Him the greatest joy.

Jesus forsook his glory and chose disgrace so that we could be redeemed from our desire for recognition and be changed into His image of humility. His lowliness, even to the point of dying like a "criminal" on the cross, is a sure guarantee of His aid for all of us who want to be free from our desire for attention.

11. Disbelief: Discouragement

"But the fearful, and unbelieving . . . shall have their part in the lake which burneth with fire and brimstone" (Rev. 21: 8 A.V.). That is the verdict God pronounces over this sin.

Why are the unbelievers struck by such a severe judgment? Why is disbelief, discouragement such a serious sin? Because, through their behaviour, they mistrust God. If a father loves his child and sacrifices everything to take care of him, can the child hurt him more than by being mistrustful and thinking, "My father doesn't intend to do anything good for me"? Jesus condemns such mistrust in the parable of the talents by replying to the servant who said, "Master, I knew you to be a hard man" (Matt. 25: 24): "Cast the worthless servant into the outer darkness; there men will weep and gnash their teeth" (Matt. 25: 30).

So it is not a harmless sin to be discouraged and to open the door to disbelief and then to persist in it. It will have terrible consequences. The kingdom of heaven will be closed for us and the door to the kingdom of darkness will open to take us in.

Then it will be of no use to try to excuse our disbelief, as we perhaps try to do now, by saying that it is hard for us to believe or even pitying ourselves for "not being able to". No, as surely as Jesus exhorts us to believe, "Have faith in God" (Mark 11: 22), we can believe. If we do not believe, it is sin. It is our pride. Pride and arrogance cause us to criticize God, by saying, "Jesus cannot help me after all. Jesus cannot forgive me! No one, not even God Himself can help me out of my need, my hopeless situation, my temptations and sins. They are too strong." When we say such things, we think we know better than God's Word which says, "Call upon me in the day of trouble; I will deliver you" (Ps. 50: 15), "I will never fail you nor forsake you" (Heb. 13: 5), "I, I am He who blots out your transgressions" (Isa. 43: 25).

It is really a symptom of great pride when we place ourselves above the Word of God with our own estimations, thoughts and judgments and think that they alone are right, arrogantly rejecting God's promises as invalid. That is why the servant, who said "Master, I knew you to be a hard man," is struck by Jesus' relentless words, which tell him that his place will be in hell, in the kingdom of Satan, who personifies hatred and mistrust.

And this judgment will strike us also, if we persist in our disbelief. We usually say so piously, "I am discouraged" instead of admitting that we are rebelling and thinking we know better than God. But if, in our pride, we act as though He cannot help us, we are insulting God, who made such a great sacrifice, delivering His Son to death on the cross to show us His love. How can we still refuse to trust His love? Because we are too proud to admit the fact that we are sinners before God and man and that we make mistakes again and again. We are also too proud to let ourselves be chastened for our sins by the fatherly love of God—just as earthly fathers chasten and discipline their children. We rebel against such discipline, although God is actually for us exactly at that moment to help us, to free us from what is causing us so much trouble: our sin. He acts in love like a Father, who chastens us so that He can give us more good things later.

Pride, mistrust and trying to evade carrying our cross are actually the reasons why we fall down. We rebel against chastening, against that which is difficult for us, and even if it is only our difficult personality and our many mistakes that humiliate us and make us ashamed. Yes, we rebel deep down in our hearts, even if we put on a different façade. We cloak our resentment when difficult things happen to us by saying "I can no longer believe in God's love." Through such mistrust we not only prevent God from working in us, but we cannot give others a testimony of faith and we deprive our service in the Kingdom of God of its power. The disciples experienced the same thing. When they asked Jesus why they did not have enough power, He had to answer, "Because of your little faith!" (Matt. 17: 20).

That is why we must fight against disbelief to the point of shedding blood. It will make us unhappy here, and one day it will make us dwell in the kingdom of darkness. No matter what it costs, we must be freed from this sin of disbelief in order to reach the goal of glory for all eternity. The first "must" in fighting against disbelief and discouragement is to pay homage to the truth and admit that we ourselves are at fault if we do not experience God's love and help. For disbelief breaks our association with God, and erects a barrier against Him, which prevents His stream of love and help from flowing towards us.

With such an attitude we should not be surprised that God's love, and all the good things that He has thought out for us, cannot flow into our hearts and lives. In the Holy Scriptures we can read the example of His people in the desert, for whom God had promised the chosen land. But we see that they could not enter due to their unbelief. That is why the Holy Scriptures exhort us, "Let us labour therefore to enter into that rest, lest any man fall after the same example of unbelief" (Heb. 4: 11 A.V.).

In order not to fall, we have to let God show us the deepest reason for our disbelief: our pride. Our next goal of faith, in order to conquer disbelief and discouragement, must be to admit before God and man that pride makes us blind to the Father's love. Only the humble will have their eyes opened to see God the Father in His infinite love. The humble will receive help. The humble and the lowly cling to God's promises. Do so!

If it becomes difficult for us to believe and we are about to become discouraged, we should pray aloud, "My Father, I do not know how You will help me, but I do know that You will help me. That is certain, for You are Love! My Father, I thank You for having a way out of this problem, for You are Love. My Father, I thank You for being greater than everything, even greater than my troubles, and for always helping me. My Father, I thank You for answering prayer and intervening. Lord Jesus, I thank You for being my Redeemer and—as surely as You keep Your word—You will free me from my chains of sin."

If we say this in humility, as His child, we will exercise our faith and will conquer our disbelief and discouragement. We must go to Him who says, "I am lowly in heart", for He has offered His sacrifice on Calvary so that we can become like Him and trust the Father with a humble heart of love—even in the midst of night. He will give us humble faith. We have been redeemed by love, trusting in the Father's goodness and faithfulness, and in the Son's complete redemption in every situation, in every trial and temptation.

12. Disobedience

Through disobedience Saul lost his kingship, although he had put so much time and energy into working for God. God is not interested in our self-chosen work and sacrifices, even when we say we are doing it for Him. When Saul clearly refused to obey the command of the Lord, Samuel reminded him that "to obey is better than sacrifice" (1 Sam. 15: 22). Obedience is pure love for God; disobedience is the selfish desire to satisfy our own egos.

If we are Christians, we usually do not act in open disobedience like non-believers. But, like Saul, we camouflage our disobedience. We say that our work is necessary, that it is a beneficial ministry for God and man. Yet whether we are believers or unbelievers, unrepented disobedience belongs to the sins that deserve death (Rom. 1: 30–32). People who dare to commit this sin reject the will of God. They have separated themselves from God and are already in death, although they may not realize it. But one day in the kingdom of death they will die a second death (Rev. 20: 14, 15; 21: 8). That is why we must turn away from all disobedience.

When we look at the people of Israel, we see the consequences of disobedience. Through disobedience the people of God turned away from God and most of the Israelites died in the desert. They did not take God's words to heart: "If you obey the voice of the Lord your God ... all these blessings shall come upon you" (Deut. 28: 1, 2). Only out of love God demanded obedience. Only out of love He gave them His commandments; and only out of love He gives us commandments today. They will lead us into good fortune if we let them be binding for us. Disobedience on the other hand, always leads us into misfortune.

Yes, disobedience, disrespect for the commandments of God which show us His will so clearly, is spreading more

widely today than ever before. And the curse of this disobedience is already manifest in all the horror of sin,
which ruins lives and leads to chaos. Does not God have
to lament again today about the many nations and especially about His own people: "All day long I have held
out my hands to a disobedient and contrary people"
(Rom. 10: 21). They "walk in a way that is not good,
following their own devices" (Isa. 65: 2). Often it is especially His own that are in danger of disobedience without their realizing it. They know His will and
commandments better than people who are separated
from God and they know how important it is for them to
listen and obey. But today there are so many "reason-
able" arguments about why the commandments of God
are not binding on us, not even for us Christians. People
say that the commandments have to be adjusted to the
conditions of the times. But if Christians are disobedient
and change the standards of the commandments in a false
manner, they will have to bear serious consequences.

There is still another form of disobedience, a "pious"
form. Many Christians spend themselves in service for
the Lord. They offer one sacrifice after another. And still
they will bear no fruit. There is no blessing in their work,
although they may be praised by many. God sees their
hearts, but men only see what is before their eyes. Because of their work in the Kingdom of God others might
praise them "to highest heaven", but in reality their place
may be very far away from God. For their sacrifices were
self-chosen; they were offered in disobedience to God.

There may have been a missionary who was sent home
from the field, because she was sick. At the mission she
had been admired for her dedication, love and willingness
to sacrifice. Back home she suddenly became unbearable,
rebelling against everything, because she had to do ad-
ministrative work. Why? She said, "I cannot live without
serving men." But then God will pronounce this verdict
over her; "To obey is better than sacrifice" (1 Sam. 15:
22). She could not humble herself in obedience to God's
will—leaving her former work because of illness. Her
ministry was not done out of love for God nor out of

pure love for man. She had lived for herself; she performed this ministry to satisfy her own ego. She was missing the true love for Jesus, for Jesus said, "If a man loves me, he will keep my word" (John 14: 23); he will do God's will.

We see how cleverly the enemy deals with us so-called "pious" Christians. He knows that we will not consciously commit an obvious sin, because we know that disobedience is a sin and will be punished severely. That is why he uses a different method to catch us in his trap. He tells us that we should sacrifice something special for God and His service, or for our neighbour in his need. But in face of the serious consequences that disobedience has for time and eternity, we should stop and ask God, "Place me in the light of Your truth. Let me see the true motives for my actions and repent when You unmask them and show me that my decisions and actions stemmed from disobedience!"

If God convicts us of disobedience and we find it difficult to be obedient to His will, we should look at the countenance of Jesus, which is pure love and tells us that His will is goodness. Jesus is asking us to accept His will and to carry it out in obedience. He assures us that only our best interests lie in His will. We hurt Jesus, if we do not believe that His heart is full of love, that His will is only goodness, and so try to frustrate His loving intentions by disobedience. Love obeys. Yes, if I love someone I can read his desires in his eyes. We are called and redeemed to have such a relationship of love to God; we are to follow in the footsteps of Jesus, who said, "My food is to do the will of him who sent me" (John 4: 34). If our heart is resting in His will, we will be filled with peace and joy. Then all our actions will bring forth eternal fruit, and God's blessing will rest upon all our ways.

When we are at one with the will of God, our lives will be filled with power, for then we are at one with Him who has all power in heaven and on earth. When we surrender our will to God, His heart will be opened and a stream of love, peace and joy will flow into our hearts. Being at one with the will of God remoulds us so that we

73

will be like Him. Words are not sufficient to express the spiritual wealth that obedience and commitment of our wills to Him will bring us. When we obediently say, Yes, to the will of God, even when it comes to us through other people, our suffering and needs will lose their power. Therefore, no matter what it costs, we must always choose God's will and not our own. In all matters, large and small, we are constantly confronted by this choice. But every time let us realize this: if we choose God's will and act according to His commandment, we will be bound to Him. But if, in disobedience, we do our own will, we will be bound to Satan. Our lives will not be blessed and this will have serious consequences in the other world.

13. Disrespect: Negation of Authority

Why is it so difficult for us to respect people who deserve to be respected? Why is it especially true in our times, even among Christians, that people take such a stand against respect and authority? Why is it difficult for us to recognize the words of Scripture and to regard them as binding for us in our everyday life: "Outdo one another in showing honour" (Rom. 12: 10) and "Count others better than yourselves" (Philip. 2: 3)? Yes, why? Because we are so filled with our own importance and our own honour. The proud cannot humble themselves easily. When I respect someone else, I humble myself before him in spirit. Then *I* have taken the lower position; I have to honour the other person, because he is above me, because he is more mature or older, because he has attained more, because he is my superior, or because he is my parent.

Only the humble can give respect. But because we often lack humility, we refuse to respect others. And only the humble will accept the truth that because they are younger, they often do not have the same degree of maturity, the same wisdom, the same rights and privileges that an older person has. Children will see that because they are like children, needing education, they are not yet old enough to take on the responsibilities and privileges of parents. Employees will see that they are not the boss, and therefore have to accept and obey the current rules, which, of course, does not mean that we should ignore our sense of responsibility. It is a matter of accepting these things. If I respect God, I also have to respect those whom He has appointed to be above me, in spite of their deficiencies and mistakes.

That would be obvious to all of us, if, yes if, the sin of pride were not in us. Satan incites it with his arguments which we like so much to hear. For instance, "We all have the same rights", or, "No one should have a position of authority above anyone else". Satan, the fallen Lucifer, *has to* argue like this. He fell, because he did not want to respect God; he wanted to be equal with Him. Now he wants to pull us men after him. He wants to make us fall also, so that we will be his prey. He does not want to let us choose Jesus' way, being humble and giving respect to others. He does not want us to become like God and reach the great glory that he lost.

Therefore, the enemy works feverishly to incite us to rebel against authorities, because he knows that then we will join him in the rebellion against God, the highest authority. Satan's poison makes us want to be equal with others, to have equal rights and equal respect. He does not want us to recognize that there are rules and superiors, that the Kingdom of God is a hierarchy, a hierarchy of reverent love. If we do not want to admit this fact, because we are exceedingly proud, we will fall into Satan's hands and fall away from God just as he did. The Word of God tells us very clearly that we must be reverent, respectful and subject to others. "Be subject to one another out of reverence for Christ" (Eph. 5: 21). "Likewise you that are younger be subject to the elders. Clothe yourselves, all of you, with humility toward one another" (1 Pet. 5: 5).

According to the divine order of life, as long as the earth exists there will always be relationships that demand the paying of respect. There will always be those who teach and those who are taught; parents, and children who need to learn many things and be brought up; employers, and employees who have to learn the trade. Otherwise the result would be chaos. If today we deny this and loudly proclaim the new anti-authoritarian society and way of life, we will actually become slaves of those leaders and authorities who come from Satan. In the end we will have to do exactly what we are fighting against: to slavishly obey the authoritarian slogans of our leaders. But God would like to grant us a new and blessed relationship of respect for one another—one that stems from voluntary love and respect of those who deserve honour.

Lack of respect, which is a result of pride, destroys the Kingdom of God in our midst and binds us tightly to Satan. Indeed, at the end of our lives it can bring us into his kingdom of darkness, where the proud and haughty live. If we do not want that to be our fate, let us recognize those whom God has placed over us and strive to be freed from our disrespect. Jesus shows us the way to be healed from pride and disrespect. We should look at Him and His humility. He said, "The Son can do nothing of his own accord" (John 5: 19) and "The Father is greater than I" (John 14: 28). By looking at Jesus, the humble Son of God, who reverently always honoured the Father, we will be remade in His image.

We must fight the battle of faith in the power of His blood, so that His virtue of reverence might gain room in us. Taking the first step, we must humble ourselves and begin concretely to respect those whom we are supposed to respect. We must obey them by doing everything they demand that is not against our consciences (Acts 5: 29), be respectful towards them, show them our esteem and gratitude. We must prove to them, through our behaviour and actions, that we are respecting Jesus in them—Jesus, our Lord, who has placed them above us.

But if we see our superiors sinning, we must ask for the humility, the courage and the proper moment to speak with them about this. Otherwise we are in danger of speaking about them behind their backs and ruining their reputation instead of being a witness for Jesus with all respect for them. Jesus wants to set us free from disrespect and at the same time from trying to please man and being servile. Because this is a narrow path, we will only find it through the power of His redemption. When we live in true reverence and respect, the hosts of heaven will surround us. For we will be following their example. The angels and the cherubim, the elders and the saints humbly bow before God and in reverence cast their crowns before the throne of God (Rev. 4: 10).

14. Egoism

Egoists are the antithesis of what we were created to be. We were created and redeemed by the Lord who is eternal Love. Jesus has freed us so that we can love. And love always centres around the other person. Egoism is the opposite of love, because the egoist just centres around himself and is not at all sensitive to the other person and what he needs or desires. While love takes care of the other person and gives freely, the egoist is only concerned about whether his own ego is satisfied. He has to have his rights. His demands have to be satisfied, whether they have to do with health, comfort, free time, rights or respect. He only lives for his ego; he pampers it. And he is not interested in the trouble he causes others, the time and energy that he steals from them. Yes, and at times he even takes advantage of the people around him quite consciously, especially those who are beneath him, and uses them in such a way that their body, soul or spirit may be harmed.

The terrible part of this is that the egoist is living for himself and not for God, and also not for his neighbours whom God has given him. Instead of worshipping God, he is actually worshipping his own ego. It will be terrible when he awakes in eternity. He will be condemned by the sharp verdict: "Outside (outside of the city of God) are the idolaters" (Rev. 22: 15). An egoist, in his inconsiderate self-centredness, is in danger of stopping at nothing to satisfy his own demands, regardless of the damage he may cause his neighbours. Thus, in many different ways, he trespasses against the commandments of God and heaps judgment and misfortune upon himself. So we must learn to hate our egoism and conduct a serious battle of faith against it, in order to be redeemed.

Above all, it is necessary to recognize our camouflaged egoism in the light of God. We can camouflage our

78

egoism, for instance, by loving our own family and taking care of them. Certainly this is actually a good thing. But if we are so interested in the rights and welfare of our family that we put others at a disadvantage, it is "family egoism". We are merely centring around an "extended ego". Another expression of this family egoism may be that parents, for the sake of more ambitious plans, try to hinder a child from following God's call to devote himself to full-time service in God's kingdom.

Egoism does not only make other people suffer and make us sin against them, it also damages our own soul. We feed it with everything that our ego desires so that there is no longer any room for divine life, for the indwelling of our Lord Jesus in our hearts. Then Jesus speaks these serious words to us; "You have the name of being alive, and you are dead" (Rev. 3: 1). If we believe in Jesus and still are ruled by egoism, we are leading an imaginary Christian life, and we belong to the hypocrites. When we gave our lives to Jesus, we gave Him first claim on our lives: "He died for all, that those who live might live no longer for themselves but for him who for their sake died and was raised" (2 Cor. 5:15).

But how many Christians have simply held on to their egoism when they became Christians and let it thrive in the spiritual domain? This cancerous growth very quickly permeates all our new spiritual interests: the yearning for quiet prayer time, for greater knowledge, for fellowship with other Christians, for preaching and worship services, and so on. Without realizing it, we go to meetings only for our own edification, not to join others in giving God the glory. Even back in the days of the early Church the Apostle Paul had to lament, "They all look after their own interests, not those of Jesus Christ" (Phil. 2: 21). The "pious" egoist judges everything according to how much he gets out of it. He sings, prays, believes and lives a "spiritual" life for his own sake, but in doing so he falls into great hypocrisy. He only needs the Lord when He can do something for him. That is why he is insolent to the Lord when the Lord does not answer his demands, but disappoints his egoistical expectations.

The egoist is a misrepresentation of Jesus' disciples. This verse applies to him, "Whoever does not bear his own cross and come after me, cannot be my disciple" (Luke 14: 27). Therefore, he cannot belong to His kingdom. He is lacking an important element of Jesus' life and the life of all true disciples: sacrifice. Only where there is sacrifice is there true love. And whoever practices the opposite of love in his life will be outside the kingdom of heaven, which is a kingdom for those who love. The egoist who spares his ego, avoids sacrifice and is thus guilty towards love will not belong to Jesus and His kingdom, either here or in eternity.

Because we are all egoistically inclined, we must clearly realize that we have to be freed from this egoism no matter what it costs. The way to this involves a definite surrender of the will. We have to make a decision. Do we want to continue to assert ourselves, and give in to our demands, longing for their fulfilment? Or do we want to hate this "idol", our ego, and cease giving it anything to nourish it? Do we want to do everything to help put it to death? If we say to Jesus, "I want to be Your disciple; I want to go the way of sacrifice with You", the first step has been taken. For Jesus can only free us from our bondage to sin, if we consciously surrender ourselves to God.

This way of dedication is clearly outlined in the Letter to the Philippians; "Let each of you look not only to his own interests, but also to the interests of others". Then Jesus' way of sacrifice is depicted: "Have this mind among yourselves, which you have in Christ Jesus, who ... emptied himself ..." (Phil. 2: 4 ff). The more we can picture our Lord Jesus and the way He went and are amazed by His love which emptied itself for us, the more we will be able to hate our ego and our egoism. Then thanks and love for Him will urge us to claim His redemption and fight the battle of faith against this sin of egoism. That means that we have to praise the power of the blood over all the demands of our ego whenever they arise in us.

But it also means that every time an egoistic act overtakes us, we should really be compelled to repent. Every time we have sided with our ego and have tried to hold on to this or that, we should let go and in addition sacrifice as much as possible. In answer to our prayers for deliverance from our egoism God will demand many painful sacrifices, and then we must say, Yes. And we should devote ourselves especially to those whom we have harmed through our egoism and thoughtlessness. Then Jesus will prove who He is and what He can do. He can turn an egoist into a loving, self-sacrificial soul, to the glory of His name.

15. Envy

Envy is a poisonous root in our soul that can kill others. Jesus Himself was delivered up to this murderous power, for it is written: Pilate "knew that it was out of envy that they had delivered him up" (Matt. 27: 18). Envious people cannot bear to see their neighbours—especially their equals or those they live with—get something more or better than themselves. That is especially true in the areas that interest us most, for instance, intellectual endowments, physical beauty and strength, or recognition and popularity, material advantages and various blessings at home or at work. For instance, it hurts the envious mother when she sees that her neighbour's child is more popular than her own, or if he has a happy marriage when her child does not. How often do we look askance, just because the other is getting along all right!

In such situations, when God has given someone else something that He has denied us, we seldom stop at just having hurt feelings. This poison oozes out of our hearts in word and deed. In the more harmless cases we are unfriendly to others; we repel them; we quarrel with them and make life difficult for them. But often—just as the Pharisees took revenge on Jesus—we take revenge on others, because they have taken honour, recognition and popularity away from us through their own popularity. We try to humiliate them somehow, to take them down a peg or two in the sight of others, or to put them out of the limelight as best we can. Sometimes we are unconscious of this, because we pretend that we have impartial reasons for fighting against them. And if we become conscious of our envy, perhaps we try to make it seem harmless or we even feel sorry for ourselves, because God has not given us something that He has given to others. If we do so, we are justifying our envy.

In our blindness we do not see that when we are filled

with envy we will come under God's serious judgment. For envy is one of the sins that can exclude us from the Kingdom of God according to the Holy Scriptures (Gal. 5: 20 f.). For the envious this means a devastating fate in the future. They will be denied entrance into the kingdom of Jesus Christ, even if they are Christians. In the face of eternity we cannot tolerate envy at any price. This poisonous, sinful root has to be eradicated if we wish to be with Jesus for ever. Because the Word of God speaks so clearly about envy, we have to take the Apostle Peter's admonition seriously: "So put away all malice and envy" (1 Pet. 2:1).

Now it is a matter of making every effort to get rid of this sin. But how? First we have to pay homage to the truth and admit that we are envious because another has something we do not have. We have to record such feelings and thoughts soberly as sins. The judgment of God is upon them. Then we will be frightened and abhor this sin and will let ourselves be shown the roots of envy. The main roots are usually in our selfishness or in our cravings, whether they be for physical or spiritual goods. Therefore, we must ask ourselves, "Are we willing to surrender our selfishness and our claims on possessions and talents to Jesus and to be poor with Him in the way of material goods, abilities, love and respect? Are we willing to believe that God will always endow the poor and that they are the ones who are really rich?"

The second root of envy is mistrust against God. It is comparing ourselves with others, as though the Father in heaven had been unjust when He distributed His gifts and burdens. Therefore, it is a matter of renouncing our rebellious, mistrustful thoughts. Instead we must trust that God, because He is Love, always gives us what is best for us. He always leads us the best way. If He had a better way for us, He would have chosen it.

No matter how He leads us, whether He gives us something or not, it is always best for us, because it comes from the hands of the Father who loves us. We must believe that firmly. Besides, we can never judge the pleasures and burdens of others, because we cannot see the background! Perhaps we envy someone for something that is merely a difficult task for them.

The third root of envy is ingratitude. Therefore we must begin to give thanks for everything that we have received, and then there will be no more room for envy. If we give thanks to God for the gifts that others receive, the poison of envy must yield.

No matter what it costs, Jesus wants to free us from envy, if we will take the first step as a sign of our willingness and surrender our envious desires to Him. He has come to burst our chains. His blood is sufficient to heal this sinful ailment. He wants to transform us until we can remain at peace in situations where, formerly, our envy would have torn us to pieces. Yes, until we can even rejoice when others have more talents than we do. When we are redeemed from this tormenting envy, we will become happy and able to taste His kingdom of peace and joy here, and one day we will dwell there eternally. Therefore, "fight the good fight of faith!" It is worth it!

16: Greed: Craving

Whenever we see something that we would like to have for body, soul or spirit, our heart begins to say, "Give me; Give me!" Even the smallest child says that. He stretches out his hand to get it just as Eve, the mother of our race, reached for the forbidden fruit.

The desire to have can either be for "more" or for "much". But it also can be a desire for the "best"; anything less is not good enough. There are many children—and sometimes adults also—whose eyes are bigger than their stomachs. They heap more upon their plates than they can eat; they always reach for the best piece. This desire for more or for especially good food is often very strong. In time of war and famine we have often seen what a power this is. People lose their dignity and break all ethical rules just to satisfy their desires.

Furthermore, all of us know how much we long for sleep and comfort. The bondage to sleep can be so great that we can sacrifice even things essential for life, even our prayer time, just in order to be able to sleep more. Our desires are kindled by many things—by modern clothing, more money, more comfort, and conveniences. But in our hearts there is not only greediness for visible goods, but also often for things that satisfy the soul; like attention, respect and love from other people.

Greed is a dangerous sin: it was the beginning of the fall. So greed can once again cost us the loss of "paradise" and the blessing of our birthright as in Esau's case. Therefore, we cannot afford to persist thoughtlessly or indifferently in greed for certain things, in bondage to food and sleep, in greed for "more"—more money, goods, talents or anything else that we desire.

For Holy Scripture says, "Those who desire to be rich fall into a temptation, into a snare, into many senseless and hurtful desires that plunge men into ruin and destruction" (1 Tim. 6: 9).

This is what greed leads to, not only for this life, but for eternity. The sin of greed not only makes us often sin against others, but it also causes us to lose our connection with God. Anything that we crave for or are attached to—other than God—is an idol. And God will not share His love with any of our idols. If we hold on to them, we will lose the love of God. Our joy in God will be taken from us. Jesus shows us the consequences in the parable of the rich man. After he had satisfied all his desires in his earthly life, his tongue burned in the other world due to unfulfilled desires and he was "in anguish" (Luke 16: 24).

Everything depends upon our being set free from greed. Jesus shows us the way by saying "Lose!". "Whoever loses his life for my sake will find it" (Matt. 16: 25). This slogan "to lose" is a weapon in the fight against desire. But beware: only if we lose things, goods, large and small, for body, soul and spirit, will we give greed a setback. We must begin to act categorically and turn away from the things we desire most at the moment. In spirit we should offer them up to God, and not spend much time thinking about them. We must not ask for them, nor help ourselves to them. And by giving them away we will no longer nourish the greed in us and it will starve to death.

For instance, if we are bound to food, we should become accustomed to eating with discipline and to praying while eating, "You have set me free from this bondage". We should look on our palate as our enemy and not let it have any especially tasty thing until it does not matter what we eat. Then we can enjoy good food with thanksgiving for the gift of God's great goodness—but we can also be satisfied with less at other times.

Similarly, if our bondage is to sleep. When we go to sleep, we should ask the Lord to wake us at the right time, or set our alarm clock so that we will have time for the Lord and prayer at the beginning of the day, or ask others to help us get up early. We must ask Jesus to be the Lord of our sleep, the Lord of our food, not we ourselves. Our limbs, our tongues, our eyes, our bodies, are to serve righteousness, to be used for His glory and not for unbridled desires, which will enslave us.

That is why the Apostle Paul emphasizes this point in his first letter to Timothy; "There is great gain in godliness with contentment" (1 Tim. 6: 6). That means, we should be contented with what we have rather than desire to have more free time and vacation, a higher salary, a better house, better clothing, etc. We must not strive for perishable things, for they often bring sin and misfortune. We should choose the way of contentedness, even the way of deprivation. For that was Jesus' way. Jesus, who possessed all the wealth in heaven and on earth, deprived Himself of the glory He had with the Father and walked the earth as a poor man. "For you know the grace of our Lord Jesus Christ, that though he was rich, yet for your sake he became poor, so that by his poverty you might become rich" (2 Cor. 8: 9). He is calling us to join Him in being content; then the promise of God's blessing will be upon us.

No man can serve two masters at the same time. No man can strive for earthly and eternal riches at the same time. Whoever seeks earthly things will lose eternal riches. But whoever seeks the Kingdom of God will reach eternal glory above and everything he needs in the way of earthly goods will be given to him by God (Matt. 6: 33).

We have to make a decision! Jesus, who went the way of deprivation and losing for our sake, has gained this new way of thinking for us, through His sacrificial death. Therefore, in faith we must take hold of the victory banner and rely upon His victory: "I have been redeemed in the blood of the Lamb from all greed and craving". Let us allow no day to go by without looking at Jesus and being set on fire to give up something instead of craving for things. Then all our desires will be satisfied in Him.

My Lord Jesus! You have been deprived of everything for me. Your joy in being content and satisfied, Your willingness to give away everything is now mine. You have paid the price on Calvary. I am free from *the powers of greed. Your love will only let one desire live in me—the desire to reach the heavenly, eternal glory.*

17: Hypocrisy

"Woe, to you, hypocrites!" This cry resounds seven times in Jesus' address to the scribes and Pharisees. "So you also outwardly appear righteous to men, but within you are full of hypocrisy and iniquity!" (Matt. 23: 28). The same is true of us Christians today. It often happens that others think we are believers, but really our hearts are full of sins such as bitterness, judging, pride, lying, strife, etc.

Jesus calls this hypocrisy. Hypocrisy is pretending to be pious when we are really not. It is an especially ugly type of deceitfulness, since piety is supposed to be a life with and for God, who is Light and Truth. That is why Jesus says the hypocrites will come under serious judgment. He tells us in advance what the terrible fate of the pious hypocrites will be: "You serpents, you brood of vipers, how are you to escape being sentenced to hell?" (Matt. 23: 33). Jesus' warning shows us that Satan, the liar from the very beginning, wants to make every effort to catch people who have escaped from him by believing in Jesus. Now he wants to catch them in the fishnet of hypocrisy without their realizing it. Satan usually succeeds very easily, because we who know Jesus Christ as our Redeemer are in danger of becoming too certain that we live for Jesus, in the realm of divine truth through the word of God. But in reality our Christian life is often just a façade. Behind it there is a different reality.

For instance, we can say that Jesus has reconciled us and we can preach reconciliation to others, and yet be unreconciled with someone, concealing bitter, critical thoughts in our hearts. We do not hear Jesus pronouncing judgment over us, "You hypocrite!" (Luke 6: 42), because He knows that we are not living what we preach.

Furthermore, the "woes" that Jesus spoke to the Pharisees will also apply to us if we hypocritically maintain that we are disciples of Jesus and yet refuse to take up our cross. We complain about every burden, need and type of suffering. We even grumble when the smallest things turn out to be unpleasant. Or we rebel when we think we are not treated well enough by people, when we are sick or other difficult things hit us. Yet Jesus has said, "Whoever does not bear his own cross and come after me, cannot be my disciple" (Luke 14: 27).

We may have a special talent for preaching and seem to be accomplishing a great deal in the souls of men, or we may put much time and energy into service and prayer for the kingdom of God. Still Jesus has to threaten us with judgment. Why? Because our ministry for Jesus was just a show. When we worked for the Kingdom of God, we were not really interested in Jesus and His honour, as people thought we were. We did not perform our ministry out of love for Him, but rather to satisfy our own ego, or to gain the admiration of others and to make a reputation for ourselves. That is, we had ulterior motives.

Yes, we can do great deeds for Jesus, perform miracles, heal the sick and still become Satan's prey, if we do not do the will of God at the same time, as Jesus clearly taught us in His interpretation of the Ten Commandments in the Sermon on the Mount (Matt. 7: 22 f.). The enemy is triumphant, if he can find criticism, slander, sensual desires, perhaps some type of licentiousness, lack of love for parents, and similar things in our lives. The greatest trick of the enemy is to keep us Christians from realizing that we are leading a two-track life.

To live hypocritically means to think that we are committed Christians, to pray much, read the Bible, be active in a Christian fellowship, perhaps even do missionary work, yet not practise what we read in the Bible, pray about and tell others to do. As hypocrites we do not realize that we have fallen into the sleep of the self-certain, who are sure that they have been saved and will go to heaven one day, while Satan laughs scornfully. To a great extent we do not practise what we preach. This is a shocking fact; it ought to shake us up. When we live such a hypocritical life, we become guilty towards our fellow men. We not only destroy the credibility of the Gospel for others, but we even cause them to reject Jesus. And we ourselves will be struck by Jesus' shocking verdict, "The hypocrites will be cast into outer darkness; there men will weep and gnash their teeth" (Matt. 24: 51). As hypocrites we will become children of hell (Matt. 23: 15).

Our hypocrisy provokes the wrath of God, because He is only pleased when we lead our everyday life according to His Word. There is scarcely any other sin that Jesus threatens to judge so severely as the sin of hypocrisy. Therefore, we have to put all our efforts into being freed from the chains of this sin.

How does this happen? First, by recognizing the root of hypocrisy. Jesus called the pious, hypocritical Pharisees "blind" (Matt. 23: 16). What were they blind about? Their weaknesses and their sins. They thought they were perfect. So whenever we think we are good Christians, we ought to be filled with holy uncertainty and ask ourselves whether we are leading a hypocritical life. If we do not want to fall into this sin, we have to ask Jesus ever anew, "Place me in the light of Your truth—reveal in Your light everything in my life that is not pure!"

To be saved from this sin and to be kept from falling into it entails asking for the light of truth over and over again. Our eyes have to be opened so that we can see our blindness, our self-certainty and sleepiness. For only if we can see our sins and be frightened by them, can we bring them to Jesus and be freed. A sick person can only be helped if he recognizes and admits that he is sick. Otherwise he would not go to the doctor and the disease would get worse and worse, and, if it is dangerous, it could lead to death. Disciples of Jesus should follow this advice: Do not be sure that you are all right. Unknown to us there may be a very serious sin in God's sight that is covered up by a pious life. Only if we have a holy uncertainty and alertness, can we deal with the danger of hypocrisy.

We will probably all experience the same thing. Whenever we bring our thoughts, words and actions into the light of truth and measure our lives quite concretely according to the standards of Holy Scripture, we will be amazed and frightened at the difference between pretence and reality in our lives. We know what is in the Scriptures, yet we do not practise it in our lives. We confuse knowledge and action. If we use the Holy Scriptures as our standards,* we will begin to hate hypocrisy and our repentance will drive us to a battle of faith to lead a genuine life of discipleship.

Being alert in our effort to live up to the standards of the Word of God, requires time for meditation. It is advisable to take one Sunday every month, or any other definite day (besides the usual daily quiet time) to settle accounts. Then we will have several hours of quiet when we can do our spiritual bookkeeping, using the commandments of God as a mirror of conscience, and asking God to test the genuineness of our discipleship. His light will fall into our imaginary world and we will recognize the truth about ourselves and will once again recognize sin for what it is.

It will also help us if we ask those around us to tell us what we do and say that is wrong. Only those who are willing to hear the truth about themselves will be freed from the sin of hypocrisy. Those who admit their hypocrisy will be compelled to go to the Physician, who alone can heal this disease: Jesus, who is the Truth. His redemption is the guarantee—if we claim it in faith—that we can be freed from all untruthfulness in our pious lives.

* It may be of help to read the pamphlet *Mirror of Conscience* by M. Basilea Schlink.

18. Impatience

Patience is listed among the fruits of the Spirit in the Holy Scriptures (Gal. 5: 22). So impatience is a fruit of the flesh, a sin, and we cannot excuse it by saying it belongs to our personality. Rather we must make a great effort to change from an impatient person into a patient one.

Again and again the Bible exhorts us to be patient. "A man of quick temper acts foolishly" (Prov. 14: 17). Because impatience is a sin and sin always makes us unhappy, we will experience the consequences. Impatience makes us liable to be defeated and incapable of mastering difficulties. Our impatience makes us hit our heads against the wall. We do not achieve anything by this, but only cause damage.

Impatient people race around as though they were riding "upon swift steeds". This is the picture the prophet Isaiah paints for us after he has admonished the people, "In quietness and trust shall be your strength". But the people did not listen to this admonition; they said, "No! We will speed upon horses". Isaiah gave the Lord's reply, "Therefore, your pursuers shall be swift" (Isa. 30: 15 f). There is nothing edifying in impatience, nothing peaceful. It only brings commotion. Yes, impatience can lead to disastrous false reactions. Against this picture of the swift steeds is set the picture of our Lord Jesus, the picture of the Lamb, who was always patient. As the patient Lamb He attained the victory. How? Jesus, the Lamb of God, was patient, because He had surrendered His life to suffering. Jesus stands before us as the Man of Sorrows, quiet as a lamb, who bore all disgrace, scorn, condemnation, chains and fetters, anguish of body and soul.

So the patient are the true disciples of Jesus. The Apostle Paul admonishes us in 1 Thess. 5: 14 (A.V.) "Be patient toward all men". And James writes, "Behold, we call those happy who were steadfast" (Jas. 5: 11). The revelation of John confirms this fact. After the angel reports about the Antichrist and how most of the people fall prey to his dominion and come under dreadful punishment, he turns to those who remained on God's side and says, "Here is the patience of the saints" (Rev. 14: 12). What dreadful consequences there will be, if we do not learn how to master our impatience in the small things of everyday life. Whoever cannot wait for the small problems to be solved will never be able to wait until God's time comes for the big ones. In trouble and affliction we reach for means that often bring us into sin. When we are sick or in need some of us are even tempted to go to sorcerers or fortune-tellers. Then our impatience, if it causes us to become involved with the occult, will lead us into Satan's snare, just as many believers who do not endure in patience will become bound to the Antichrist in the last times.

We have to begin to learn patience today, before we enter the great tests of patience. The first step is to commit ourselves to the Lord to be patient and wait for the hour when God will come with His help. Only those who are willing to wait can be patient. It involves suffering, if we have to wait for a long time until God's help comes. Even in small things, it is difficult for us, if we cannot have our own way, if we cannot attain what we want, or if things do not happen the way we want them to at that minute. It involves suffering, if we continually have to wait for things and are continually disappointed.

It also involves suffering, if our bondages are not broken quickly or if we do not attain our goals of faith as soon as we wanted. That can apply to ourselves or to others for whom we are praying. We have to take a stand against this "spiritual" impatience, which can quickly develop into discouragement and rebellion. Otherwise we can ruin our whole spiritual life. The Holy Scriptures often speak of "growth" in spiritual life. Just as we can hinder the growth of a plant by impatiently trying to hurry it along, so we can also harm spiritual growth by impatience. Here too it depends upon the humble commitment of our wills to the leadings of God, patiently keeping faith; and faith will never let us perish.

The key to being able to endure patiently is the sure faith that God will never come too late. When His time arrives, help will come mightily. God is Love, and His love will surely come. Therefore, I can wait patiently. The knowledge that God's will is behind everything, even behind all frustrating circumstances which seek to make us impatient, will help us practise patience in everyday life. God's will is behind all the decisions of our superiors, unless they ask us to do something against our conscience. The minute we give up our self-will and commit ourselves to the will of God, trusting in His love, we can bear the situation patiently.

In practice that means consciously committing our wills to the Lord for all the frustrations, difficulties, delays, etc., that the day will bring; and all day long, whenever impatience seeks to get its hold on us in difficult situations, we must believe that every situation comes from God.

Again let us picture Jesus, who always completely yielded His will to God and therefore could be patient in all trouble and suffering. His love for the Father enabled Him to do this and let Him acquiesce to His Father's will. He, the Lamb, yielded His will and won the victory over all opposing powers. Through patience Jesus proved that He was the strong Lord, who conquered hell and Satan.

Love and trust in the Father make us strong to go the way of patience. Only then do we prove we are true disciples who are following the Lamb on His way. This way will end in glory. All who bring forth the fruits of the Spirit, including patience, will inherit the Kingdom of God, in contrast to those who bring forth the fruits of the flesh. So the fruit of patience has to be found in our life. And if we are very impatient by nature, we have to take up the fight between flesh and spirit (Gal. 5: 17) until we have overcome.

For Jesus says, "He who conquers shall have this heritage" (Rev. 21: 7). If we proclaim the name of the Victor and Redeemer ever anew over our sin of impatience, we will become more and more transformed into the image of Jesus, the patient Lamb of God. For this He has redeemed us with His precious blood.

19. Indifference: Lukewarmness

"Because you are lukewarm, and neither cold nor hot, I will spew you out of my mouth" (Rev. 3: 16). This terrible word of judgment applies to an indifferent, lazy person. Scarcely anything makes an impression on him. If problems are created, if others come into difficulties due to his fault, an indifferent person will scarcely take notice of it. He goes back to his normal routine without noticing what he has done. If everything depends upon doing something on behalf of the Lord's work and giving a testimony, he does not realize what is going on and so he misses his chance. If a brother next to him is sinning or is about to fall away from the Church, he is not stirred at all. He does not plead for the salvation of others in prayer. His whole prayer life is lukewarm. His heart is scarcely moved when God has to judge the Church or when the name of the Lord is slandered. He hardly perceives it. He does not really care what happens around him.

Indifference is spiritual death. But we seldom recognize this. We go to church or to Christian meetings, we faithfully take our part, but the Lord pronounces His verdict, "You have the name of being alive, and you are dead" (Rev. 3: 1). Love, the sign of spiritual life, the only thing that matters in God's sight, is missing. An indifferent person is usually deaf to Jesus' concerns and requests, because only a loving heart could perceive such concerns. He is not aglow with love, nor on fire for His kingdom, nor does he spend himself in sacrifice for the Lord's work.

If we are indifferent, we are just going along for the ride in Christian groups, and this grieves our Lord very deeply. We can hear Him lamenting over the indifferent, "Would that you were cold or hot!" Jesus laments so deeply, because He cannot find the one thing His heart longs for so much, love, which is warm and aglow, and which cannot do enough for Him, even if it costs a great deal. Yes, love is zealous; it presses forth. Love is full of life; love sacrifices lavishly. Without this love for Jesus we are not true disciples.

But Jesus is not only lamenting about the indifferent and the lukewarm; no, He is also threatening to spew them out of His mouth (Rev. 3: 16). A terrible judgment is awaiting the indifferent. Jesus wants to have nothing to do with them. They will be like the five foolish virgins who stood before the closed door and had to hear Jesus say to them. "I do not know you!" For the indifferent, although they have not committed any sinful acts, have sinned against God Himself. They have denied Him their love. We can only serve God with burning love, with complete devotion of time and energy, with willingness to sacrifice and with a fervent heart. Otherwise we would be disgracing Him, the Lord and King of all kings. If we work for someone who is highly respected, we would not dare to be lazy about our work. Therefore, woe unto us, if we try to do this to God. The indifferent will be struck by God's terrible words, "Cursed is he who does the work of the Lord with slackness" (Jer. 48: 10). Is there anyone who wants to be cursed by God when he knows that this can bring him continuous misfortune here on earth and dreadful judgment in eternity when he is cast into Satan's kingdom? And who wants to increase Jesus' sorrow about a world full of rebellion through his indifference? For long ago it was the indifference of His disciples, who did not understand His suffering and react in love—and today it is our indifference which wounds Jesus' heart more than does open opposition.

We must get rid of our indifference. It is such a serious sin in God's eyes. We have to regard it as our worst enemy, which will bring us into destruction, into the kingdom of darkness, full of torment and horror. We have to fight against it. We have to beseech Jesus and call to Him who has abolished death, and believe that He, Life Himself, can and will awaken us to divine life. But at the same time we must commit ourselves to being "shaken up" by God's chastening hand, which will arouse us from our indifference.

Often we can only be aroused from our indifference by thunder and lightning. Then we begin to move; then we begin to come alive. Being "shaken up" by blows of judgment is often the only treatment that works in the fight against indifference. But we have to reach for treatment. Therefore, the indifferent and lazy person has to affirm wholeheartedly God's thunder and lightning when they strike him. Judgment is the best cure. It will make us wake up from our lukewarmness and indifference. When we are judged, we will be frightened by our sin and will learn to weep over it and lament. As pardoned sinners we can do nothing else but love Jesus and spend ourselves for Him.

Sinners who lie prostrate at the cross of Jesus and receive His gifts of divine life and forgiveness, are those who love Jesus and give Him their thanksgiving and commitment.

God's judgments and chastening are the best medicine for our indifference, for they can make us contrite sinners, who cry over their sins. They can make us come alive. Therefore, let us thank Jesus for abolishing death, even the spiritual death of indifference, and for giving us release and life in such ways. Let us surrender ourselves to Him and His chastening love so that He can save us from the terrible curse that awaits the indifferent. And let us believe Jesus. He sets us free from bondage!

20. Ingratitude

Ingratitude—an ugly trait! Especially when it is directed against someone who has made sacrifices for us and done many good things for us. Our ingratitude can hurt such people deeply. What sorrow there is in Jesus' words when only one of the ten lepers that were healed came back to thank Him. "Were not ten cleansed? Where are the nine? Was no one found to return and give praise to God except this foreigner?" (Luke 17:17, 18).

But today our ingratitude is even more serious, because we actually do not appreciate the gift that surpasses all understanding—Jesus' forgiveness and His vicarious atonement for us. His sacrifice for us reveals that we as sinners need the redemption of Jesus and that we in no way have deserved love from God. Because everything we receive from God is undeserved, including what He lets other people give us, it should be a matter of course for us to thank Him. But, if we do not give thanks for His grace and undeserved gifts, we are like parasites and we should not be amazed when the wrath of God comes upon us.

Ingratitude is a serious sin. The Holy Scriptures say that it is one of the characteristics of the antichristian spirit of the last times (2 Tim. 3: 2). It will be judged severely by God. Therefore, we have to overcome all the ingratitude in our hearts if we are to belong to Jesus in eternity. We have to see what an ugly trait it is. We must be resolute and not tolerate it any longer, because it hurts the Father's heart so deeply and provokes His wrath against us.

How can we overcome our ingratitude? Here too we must first recognize the root. Just like many other sins, its root lies in pride. The proud taken it for granted that people will give them things. Consciously or unconsciously they think they have a right to receive gifts. Their eyes are blind towards all the good things that the heavenly Father gives them. In their pride they think, even when they are not consciously aware of it, that they have the right to enough, or more than enough, nourishment, clothing and everything else they need for body and soul in this life. But if they do not have sufficient goods of this life, all of a sudden they remember God and accuse Him for not giving them what they need. Their attitude towards God is like that of a person who has a lawful claim upon someone else. The ungrateful do not see that it is grace, pure grace, when God gives them what they need. So we have to humble ourselves before God and ask Him to forgive us for our pride, which kept us from thanking Him. And we have to ask for a deeper repentance over our proud ingratitude.

Then we have to take the next step by beginning to record all the good things we receive, either every day or every week. That means not only realizing this in our hearts, but bringing the Father a song or prayer of thanksgiving. It also helps when we have a special "thanksgiving booklet" in which we write down everything we receive. Then at the end of the day, or at the end of the week, either alone or with our family, we can give thanks to God. In this way our hearts practise seeing what good things we have received, from other people as well as God.

Remembering the goodness of God and the kindness of men is the first step to gratitude. Along this road we will come to realize more and more deeply that God is a Father full of love who rejoices in doing us good (Jer. 32: 41). Overwhelmed by this love, our hearts will be filled more and more with gratitude and joy. For grateful people also have good reason to rejoice over God's proofs of love, while ungrateful people are dissatisfied and upset. That is a typical symptom of pride. But the more the Lord shows us our wretchedness and sinfulness the more our hearts will rejoice when the Father in heaven, in spite of all our sins, still gives us good gifts, and people also give us presents. More and more will we learn to give thanks for even His difficult leadings, because we have come to know that His heart of love is behind them. This heart is revealed to the grateful. "Give thanks in *all* circumstances", says Scripture, "for this is the will of God in Christ Jesus for you" (1 Thes. 5: 18).

God wants to turn us into grateful people! God calls into existence things—including our gratitude—that do not exist. He will form in us new creations, grateful hearts that will also be humble, joyful and loving. The grateful are always loving. They want to repay those who have done good things for them and made them happy. What a divine radiance lies upon the grateful; the radiance of the kingdom of heaven, for above we will give thanks to God and adore Him without end for all the good that He has done for us. But we will only be there if we have learned how to give thanks here.

Is there anyone who would like to close the door to heaven for himself by being ungrateful? If not, fight the good fight of faith against the sin of ingratitude, and heaven, where joy and love reign, will be opened for you here on earth.

21. Irreconciliation: Bitterness

When people live together in reconciliation, there is peace and joy, a bit of paradise. But in a house where people have bitter thoughts in their hearts about each other, where they quarrel and do not forgive, there is a bit of hell. We know how seldom we find homes that are like a bit of paradise. For irreconciliation and bitterness are widespread sins especially among the pious.

Yet when we look at the Sermon on the Mount, this fact is completely incomprehensible. Jesus said that there would be severe punishment for those who have anything in their hearts against their brothers. He exhorts us to reconcile ourselves with our brothers at all costs, because otherwise there would be terrible consequences (Matt. 5: 23–26). The Lord says they will be put in "prison". Expressed in other words, they will come into the kingdom of darkness where men will weep and gnash their teeth. And the Apostle Paul writes in Rom. 1: 29, 32 that those who are full of strife deserve to die. In another place the implacable are listed among other objectionable types of men who will come under the wrath of God (2 Tim. 3: 3).

Christians, who actually should not come under judgment, are threatened by judgment and punishment, yes even hell, if they refuse to be reconciled. But does anyone believe this? Does anyone hate this sin and want to break away from it? Does anyone believe the words that Jesus spoke? They are true and He will act according to them. We usually do not believe them, because we say that Jesus is merciful. Perhaps we argue like this: Jesus knows our hearts; He knows how difficult it is for us to forgive someone who has hurt our feelings or wronged us unjustly or has said something about us that would ruin our reputation or hurt our family. We imagine that Jesus understands that we cannot deal with such a bitter root in our hearts. We think He understands us when we wake up at night and keep seeing these people before our eyes, and we begin to hurl one accusation after another at them.

Yes, there is probably no one who knows and understands us as well as Jesus does. He knows our sins and bondages; He calls Himself the merciful High Priest. Still He pronounces a sharp verdict over people who do not live in reconciliation, who are filled with bitterness and accusations. He does this precisely because He is our merciful High Priest, who has forgiven all our sins. Because we have received so much mercy through Him, His anger is aroused when we are not merciful to others. We can no longer dodge the issue. This fact is unmistakable in the story of the unmerciful servant. If the Lord forgives us our sins a thousand times, it is a matter of course that He will take back His forgiveness and hold us accountable again for all our sins, if we do not forgive others. Yes, His anger will judge us and throw us into the place of torment (Matt. 18: 34).

Bitterness and irreconciliation are sins which cry to heaven, since the voices of those whom we do not want to forgive reach God's heart and accuse us. God's answer will strike us like lightning: "Bind this servant who dares to be unforgiving when I have forgiven him." Who will bind him? The fallen angels who will take him and throw him into prison, into outer darkness, as Jesus describes it in another text (Matt. 22: 13).

Bitterness and irreconciliation arouse the greatest wrath of the Lamb of God. Jesus has promised us forgiveness through His blood sacrifice, although He could have accused us for our sin and everything we have done to Him.

Irreconciliation and bitterness close the heart of God to all our pleas.

Irreconciliation and all our accusations against our brothers do not only set up a barrier against our brother, but also a barrier against God.

So the motto for our life must be to live in reconciliation and bury our accusations. Otherwise we will be accused and condemned and have to live with the irreconciled in the kingdom of darkness.

How can we get rid of our bitter, accusing thoughts and reactions? By letting the light of God fall upon us and show us that we accuse others of the very things for which we ought to accuse ourselves. It will show us that we have disappointed others in the same areas they disappoint us. We have made life difficult for them also. And so we will lose our desire to accuse our brother and persist in bitterness, a sin which binds us to Satan, the accuser. We cannot rest until the Lord gives us a repentant heart about this sin of bitterness. Through repentance our accusations melt away, irreconciliation and bitterness are dissolved and we begin to see, where formerly we were blind.

If we have something in our heart against another, or we know that someone has something against us, and we are not living in reconciliation, let us speak with him, if it is possible. Whether he accepts our outstretched hand is his business. The important point is that we have a humble heart and genuine love for our opponent. In this love there is great power to change others and establish a relationship of reconciliation. Tomorrow it may be too late to be reconciled with a neighbour who may have hurt us. If we have intentionally passed by the chance for reconciliation, the accuser will take us into his kingdom. Whenever we have bitter, accusing thoughts, we live in unison with him. Immediate action is necessary if we are living in irreconciliation. We must renounce our accusing thoughts at once and fight a battle of faith against them to the point of shedding blood.

But Jesus has come to destroy the works of the devil in our soul: bitterness, accusations, irreconciliation. Jesus sent us the Holy Spirit, who wants to pour out the merciful love of God into our hearts. Whoever believes this will experience it, if he endures in faith, that is, if he does not grow weary of calling upon the victorious name of Jesus daily for the sake of His redeeming blood.

As surely as God is Yea and Amen, we will truly be freed, according to Jesus' promise that He will free us from the power of sin.

22. Jealousy

Jealousy can become such a burning desire in a person's heart that it can shrivel him up. When we are jealous, we usually torment the person we love. Yes, jealousy can give birth to hatred, betrayal and in some cases to murder. Infinite misery and sorrow have grown out of this root of jealousy. It can disrupt family life, business life and even life within our churches.

If we are not redeemed from this sin of wanting others to love us alone, we will become spiritually bankrupt and our lives will not produce any fruit. For if jealousy rules in us, we are incapable of wholeheartedly working for God and His kingdom.

We have to be freed from this sin of jealousy, no matter how high is the price. With its burning, consuming fire, it is a foreshadow of how such hellish craving can eat away at body and soul one day in the kingdom of darkness.

But God's love wants to protect us from this. Jesus through His redemption wants to free us from jealousy even if it burns like fire in our hearts. But redemption involves a genuine battle of faith on our part against this ravaging sin.

It is a matter of making a conscious renunciation of such sinful craving: "I do not want to have anything, my God, that You do not give me. If you do not give me the love of this person, I do not want to have it. I will give him up to You." God can only help us if we give up this person and our claim to his love again and again, and really lay them on the altar. Otherwise we are like a patient who has the best medicine, but still will not recover, because he does not want to leave the surroundings which are responsible for his illness and which continually make it worse. So it means completely letting go of the person whose love and attention we jealously seek. That means, we should not make any claims on him or on his time, nor should we seek to control whom he spends his time with or whom he likes.

Jesus can only set us free if we really want to be free, and give Him a sign of our willingness. Otherwise the rope that binds us to a person will bind us more and more to Satan and his kingdom. Everything is at stake. Such jealousy is a sign that we do not really love Jesus and that we are "of the flesh". "For while there is jealousy and strife among you, are you not of the flesh, and behaving like ordinary men?" (1 Cor. 3: 3). The Holy Scriptures pronounce a terrible verdict on the works of the flesh. People committing these sins will not enter the Kingdom of God (Gal. 5: 20f).

But if we have received a holy fear of our jealousy through a revelation of what jealousy really is, and we regret that we have sinned, it will lose its power over us. Then the blood of the Lamb, which makes us free from all sin will reveal its power more and more. If this redeeming blood of Jesus is proclaimed over the sin of jealousy again and again, it has power to free us. Jesus is mightier than the powers in us. His victory has condemned them to death. Whenever these sinful attachments are crucified with Christ, Jesus gives birth to new, divine love in our soul, which is free from attachments to people and cravings for human love. It will make us and others happy. Jesus has won this love for us. He wants to give it to those who are willing to surrender their sinful love and claim in faith the righteousness and love of Jesus. Only those who have overcome in their fight with sin will enter the City of God and His glory.

23. Love of Power: Desire to Dominate

"We do not want this man to reign over us!" (Luke 19: 14). This was the reason why we people killed Jesus. We wanted to reign by ourselves and not be subject to anyone else. Envy and the love of power are the main sins which nailed Jesus to the cross. This is the worst thing that could be said about any sin. The lust for power is murderous. It tramples down everyone who tries to stand in its way. Whoever persists in this sin will come under God's severe judgment, because every time we want to rule we are actually rebelling against God and His dominion. We do not leave Him any room in our lives, just as the people of Israel and its authorities did not. They excluded their Lord and Creator from their midst—just as we do when we want to have power—although His dominion was pure love and still is today.

The love of power is connected with pride and conceit. It is the characteristic of bad rulers. Domineering is expressed by bossing others around and insisting upon having our own way. It shows that we do not have any humility at all. For when we try to rule over others, we have taken a position that does not belong to us. With our love of power we set ourselves up on a throne, high above all others and rule them with our words and our deeds. But we do not realize that our attitude is just the opposite to God's attitude. For God reigns in a different way, through serving love, as Jesus practised it among men. Jesus' power was not violent; the authority of His dominion rested on humble serving love. "I am among you as one who serves" (Luke 22: 27). That is why divine radiance rested upon Jesus and why it rests upon His followers who live their lives in humble, serving love. They have true power according to Jesus' words, "Blessed are the meek, for they shall inherit (and rule) the earth" (Matt. 5: 5).

But because Jesus, the Son of God, went the way of humble, meek love, of serving others and submitting Himself, in order to redeem us from our sins, the love of power is an especially serious sin.

We are particularly vulnerable to this sin when we have a position of leadership, when we are responsible for others, even if it is the responsibility of parents for their children. Children defy their parents, rebel against them and even leave home. How often is this caused by parents who wanted to rule over them! That is why the Apostle Paul says, "Fathers, do not provoke your children, lest they become discouraged" (Col. 3: 21). "Fathers, do not provoke your children to anger, but bring them up in the discipline and instruction of the Lord" (Eph. 6: 4). Certainly parents, teachers and superiors cannot avoid making rules and making sure that things are right and if they are not, putting them back in order. But it is especially the leaders who make the Gospel unbelievable when they begin to thirst for power. The Apostle Peter admonishes the elders of the Church, "Tend the flock of God . . . not as domineering over those in your charge . . . Clothe yourselves with humility" (I Pet. 5: 2, 3, 5b).

We have to choose. Do we want to follow Satan, who wanted to usurp God's throne, even though he was created by Him? Or do we want to follow Jesus? The outcome of each of these ways is clear. Being Jesus' disciple is incompatible with thirst for power. So we have to get rid of this sin, if we wish to be counted followers of Jesus and not be excluded from His kingdom one day.

First of all, we must ask the Holy Spirit to show us our desire to rule, if we have not recognized it yet. We should ask our neighbours if we make life hard for them by our domineering attitude. If they say we do, we must accept it.

Second, we should ask for a repentant heart, for "godly sorrow" because of this malicious sin, which is such a strong contrast to Jesus' humility. Besides this we have made life difficult for those around us, yes we can even make life hell for them!

Third, we must meditate much on Jesus, the humiliated

Lord, crowned with the crown of thorns, who had love's power, and pray: "I want to stand here by You and from now on choose Your place of humble, meek love. I want others to rule over me at home and at work, and be subject to them and even give up some of my special positions and privileges."

Then we will find that our sceptre of domination will crumble in our hands and one day it will completely disappear, if, yes, if we daily entreat Jesus to free us from this sinful bondage. When we pray for this, we should constantly look at the picture of the humble, lowly Lord, who was scourged and crowned with a crown of thorns. He has paid the ransom and has gone the way of lowliness to draw us into His nature of humility. Just as we all have sinned in Adam, because as his children we partake of his sinful nature—including the love of power—so we have all been united with Jesus and His nature of humility through His redemption. Then we will find out how much authority humility has!

24. Lust

We all know the power of lust, which is in our flesh. Eve lusted for the fruit. David lusted for the wife of Uriah. Is there anyone among us who does not know how lust can suddenly arise in our hearts? We think, for example, that we cannot live, if we cannot satisfy our desire for the other sex, for a certain person. This lust arises from time to time in our blood. It has an overpowering force which is unwilling to be confined within the limits of the commandments of God, and through it sin upon sin is born. "Desire when it has conceived gives birth to sin" (Jas. 1: 15a): adultery, theft, murder.

The power of sensual desires, when people give in to them, can make them so blind that they completely disregard the commandments of God. The consequence is unbridled sexual indulgence, premarital and extramarital intercourse or sexual relations with members of the same sex. Such behaviour is almost taken for granted today. But the judgment of God is upon it, for Scripture says: "God will judge the immoral and the adulterous" (Heb. 13: 4b). "No immoral or impure man ... has any inheritance in the Kingdom of Christ and of God. Let no one deceive you with empty words, for it is because of these things that the wrath of God comes upon the sons of disobedience" (Eph. 5: 5, 6). They will weep and lament in Satan's kingdom, the kingdom of torment.

The enemy knows how to cover up the curse that lies in indulging in our lust, by trying to justify the lust in our flesh: "God, the Creator, has laid this desire in our blood; we have to satisfy it, otherwise we will not have a well-rounded personality." In reality, however, to indulge in unbridled lust leads to ruin. Certainly our sexuality belongs to the creation of God and when we practise it in the sight of His holiness, with discipline according to His commandments, we will experience His blessing. But there is scarcely any other gift of God which is so terribly misused as this one. Here the devil has found an open door. We think indulging in our desires will bring us the happiness for which we long. But apart from the Creator, and in disobedience towards Him, lust will lead us into ruin, because it brings us under Satan's dominion.

The consequences of seeking to satisfy our desires by drinking, taking drugs or indulging in sex are dreadful. If we do so, we could literally experience our bodies' decay. Many drug addicts die from overdoses, or they end up in mental institutions. People want to "enjoy" life; so they drink the cup of poison that the enemy offers them. Body and soul become poisoned; they have to suffer dreadfully and are finally destroyed—here in earthly life and then in the next world in dreadful torment.

This is a law, for sin always gives birth to death. We think we can get more out of life when we satisfy our lust, but actually we just get death. This will be revealed in a horrible way in eternity. There everyone will be able to see on our bodies just how much we have given in to our desires, and some shall awake "to shame and everlasting contempt" (Dan. 12: 2). In hell the members of our bodies that indulged in sin (for instance, the tongue of the rich man, Luke 16: 19–24) will burn, without ever being totally burned up. The desires will continue to burn in our bodies but instead of satisfaction we will experience dreadful torment.

No matter how high the price, the sinful factor in our urges, that leads us into indulgence and fornication, has to be put to death here on earth. We have to turn away from it immediately and begin to fight the battle of faith today, for we never know whether tomorrow will still come. If we are suddenly called away from this life, we may find ourselves today suffering heartache, torture and torment in the kingdom of darkness. The Word of God warns us many times about extramarital sexual relationships and sharply condemns every sexual relationship with members of the same sex. "Immorality, impurity, licentiousness ... those who do such things shall not inherit the kingdom of God" (Gal. 5:19, 21). "Neither the immoral, nor idolaters, nor adulterers, nor homosexuals ... will inherit the kingdom of God" (1 Cor. 6: 9, 10). "Shun immorality ... the immoral man sins against his own body. Do you not know that your body is a temple of the Holy Spirit within you, which you have from God? You are not on your own; you were bought with a price. So glorify God in your body" (1 Cor. 6: 18–20).

We cannot tolerate the sin of lust in any area of our lives. It must be brought into the light at once, confessed and renounced. We have to break from this sin, other-wise Satan will hold us in his chains and we will not get loose. But that is not all that is necessary. Because these urges are so deeply rooted in us, we have to begin a daily battle of prayer, and praise the redeeming power of Jesus' blood over our sin-infested blood. Part of this battle of prayer is that we confront in faith the cry of our hearts; "We want to live and satisfy our desires" with a clear resoluteness; "We want to die to our lust; we want to be crucified with Jesus and arise with Him to new life and inherit glory."

Is there any other way to come to the joy-filled life that we all long for except by dying? Even in nature we can see this law at work "Die and come to life!" All life is born out of death. Should there be any other way for us men who are so laden with sin and guilt?

The first step must be taken in our thought-life. Lust has to be confronted immediately and fought against, as soon as it appears in our thoughts. People are often tor-mented by impure thoughts, feelings and fantasies even in their dreams. Let this be our practical guide: Do not read anything in magazines, look at anything on tele-vision or listen to anything on the radio that could nourish such impure, lustful thoughts, feelings or fan-tasies. If we do not leave them alone, we will not become free. We will have to reap what we have sown, by letting all these things come into our hearts and thoughts. Here they torment us and will not let us go, and one day a terrible punishment will await us.

But whoever consistently refuses to look at impure things, or listen to them, and always claims the blood of the Lamb for that which is in his feelings and thoughts, will experience that he will be set free.

That is also true when our desires are unduly directed at a certain person. Above all we must not let ourselves be deceived by the enemy's arguments, such as: friendship with a married person is allowed because his spouse cannot offer him what he needs. The needs of the person justify the situation, and so on. We must unmask the camouflage of this temptation and then in practice avoid meetings where we might possibly encounter him, even if it is painful to make such a sacrifice. Or we have to tear up letters or pictures, if they bind us ever anew to a person and make us lust for him.

Jesus Himself tells us how important it is to fight a radical battle for eternity. He exhorts us to pluck out our eye, if it causes us to sin through evil glances. But after the exhortation comes an even more cutting word, "It is better that you lose one of your members than that your whole body go into hell" (Matt. 5: 29). The punishment for the immoral and adulterous which the Letter to the Ephesians (5: 5, 6) so earnestly speaks of is damnation into hell where we will be dreadfully tormented by Satan, the lord of hell.

That is why, if we are chained by this sin, we have to listen to Jesus' warning, "Fear Him (God, the Judge) who can destroy both soul and body in hell" (Matt. 10: 28).

We must radically turn away from all indulgence in our lust, which is a trespass against the commandments of God. In the blood of the Lamb there is power to free us from the chains of sin. Jesus' name is Redeemer. Indeed, He *is* a Redeemer and that is why He will redeem us from the fetters of sin, which bind us to Satan. Whoever makes a thorough break with his desires in faith in Jesus will experience that Jesus has come to give us life and complete satisfaction. He will thoroughly develop all the gifts of our body, soul and spirit. He will make us completely happy. He will give us the divine radiance of a loving, joyous, natural personality. Jesus is the essence of life. He alone can give us the fullness of life—only He. That is why we have to dare to act according to His words. Renounce everything; that is, forgo what we desire and what our lustful desires yearn for; leave them and hate them, insofar as they go against the commandments of God. Then we will experience that such death is the entrance gate to a joy-filled life, where we will receive the abundance of divine life, which is in Him.

In Jesus' sufferings we can see the deadly curse of all sensual lust; we can see its dreadful manifestations on Jesus' body. The picture of our Saviour, scourged and crucified, is a sermon for us; Jesus had to lay down His life for us, because we do not want to lay down our lives. We are full of desire and lust. He had to offer His body up as a sacrifice, because we so often misuse our bodies, indulge in lust and disregard the limits that God has set in His word. He had to suffer so much, because we, through such sin, disfigure the image of God, although He created and redeemed us to bear this image.

Now Jesus is asking us; "Trusting in My sacrifice, dare to lay down your life and believe that I will give you the full life!"

25. Lying: Secretiveness

". . . all liars, their lot shall be in the lake that burns with fire and brimstone" (Rev. 21: 8). Perhaps we are amazed at this verdict. But how could it be otherwise, for Satan is the "father of lies" (John 8: 44)? So all those who lie will come into his kingdom. That is why Jesus says to the Pharisees, whom He accused of lying, "How are you to escape being sentenced to hell?" (Matt. 23: 33). If Jesus places so much weight upon the sin of lying, if it will bring us into the kingdom of Satan, then we have to fight against it to the point of shedding blood and not give it any right to exist in our lives. It is a matter of being alert at the onset of the sin, when we begin to lie by twisting the facts, or exaggerating, or not wanting to bring our mistakes into the light and trying to cover them with silence or pretences. Covering up the facts begins when we only say half-truths, trying to protect our reputation.

Lies belong to the kingdom of darkness and usually go hand in hand with secretiveness. We usually say and do things secretively when our consciences tell us we should not, and when others would be right in accusing us. Because we do not want to break with our sin, we do not want anyone to discover the bad things we have done. That is why we do them in secret and do not want them to be revealed; we do not want to be judged.

Every time we do something in secret, because we do not want others to see what we are doing wrong, we have begun to lie. Then, if we are trapped, we try to get out of it by lying. That is why we should be careful not to do the slightest thing secretively. When we are tempted to do so, we must ask ourselves immediately: "Why should I not do it in front of others?" The answer is probably because there is something wrong about it. When the Jews accused Jesus, He answered, "I have spoken openly to the world . . . I have said nothing secretly" (John 18: 20).

Jesus could say this. He stands before us in His divine

majesty. He is Light and Truth, and every true disciple of Jesus ought to be able to say, "Everything that I have said and done in my life can be heard and seen by everyone. I have said and done nothing in secret, because everything I have done was done in the sight of God."

Yes, Jesus is Light. That is His glory. His nature is pure light and truth. He has redeemed us to be children of light so that all our words and actions might be pure and transparent. If we speak and act in the sight of God, we will not do anything secretively, but will only do what can stand in the light of God. On the other hand, Satan is the liar, the lord of the kingdom of darkness. If we speak and act in the dark, secretly, and do not want our words and deeds to come into the light, we belong to Satan. So we are constantly confronted with small, hidden situations that make us decide between light and darkness. Jesus' words are very serious, "For every one who does evil hates the light, and does not come to the light, lest his deeds should be exposed. But he who does what is true comes to the light, that it may be clearly seen that his deeds have been wrought in God" (John 3:20, 21).

We cannot remind ourselves of this often enough, because Satan in his craftiness always tries to tell us that covering up our sins is harmless. He sees to it that we cover up the truth before God and man, even before ourselves, and so make room for lies. We say we did not mean it that way. When we are criticized we give other motives for our actions but these motives are not the true ones. We repress the true facts and are not conscious of the fact that we are on the way to lying, or that our lives are already riddled with lies. We lie out of fear, out of pride, out of desire to please our fellow men, and for other reasons.

But Jesus has redeemed us from these dark powers of secretiveness and lying and therefore He is waiting for us to claim this redemption and run to attain the prize (I Cor. 9: 24): the City of God.

The City of God is utterly light. Liars will find its doors closed. That is why the apostles always say that we should be children of light and that light does not associate with darkness (Eph. 5: 8–13). Light and darkness, truth and lies are mutually exclusive. If we are untruthful and secretive, we are excluded from the kingdom of light, from the Kingdom of God, as Scripture tells us (Rev. 21: 27). No matter what it costs, we must make a complete break with the kingdom of darkness, the kingdom of lies. Otherwise we will lose our inheritance in the Kingdom of God, the fellowship of believers, and above all the fellowship with Jesus.

How do we become free from our disposition and inclination to do things secretively and to lie? The first step is to ask the Lord to show us the extent of this sin, which is satanic by its very nature, and to help us to abhor it. If we do not abhor it, we could very well manage to put up with it, and will not be interested in fighting against it. But we have to fight against it and not let it exist any longer. How can we do this? By unmasking the lies that we speak in haste, we deprive this sin of its powers over us. This happens when we immediately confess them to our own humiliation. Bringing them into the light sentences the sin of lying to death. Light has won and the humiliation has taken us out of Satan's sphere of influence, for he can only attack the proud and the haughty.

We have to apply the same tactics if we have done something secretly. We must unmask it and call it by name. If we have taken something away, we cannot put it back secretly, but, when we put it back, we must admit that we took it. But that's not the end. That only takes care of the sinful act. The sinful trait, lying, covering things up which is deeply rooted in us, will continue to live in us and when the appropriate situation materializes, it will manifest itself again. If we hate everything in us that is untruthful and if we sense that lies separate us from Jesus, we cannot do anything but call upon Jesus day by day—Jesus who is the Truth. Through His sacrificial death on Calvary He *did* nail the sin of lying to the cross and free us from it. It can no longer rule over us, because He has trodden it under His feet. Jesus, the Truth, reigns in us.

"I am redeemed; I have been set free for the truth!" That is how we should begin our battle of faith every day. And what we believe will come to pass. No matter how much we are inclined to lie, if we carry out this battle of faith, Jesus will make us utterly truthful, so that we can enter the city of light as children of light.

26. Mercilessness: Hard-Heartedness

When we think of the sin of mercilessness, we usually think of a hard-hearted person, that coldly refuses to listen to pleas for help from the needy. That is wrong, because it is one-sided. Mercilessness includes something else that pertains to us all: "passing by". We do not need to do anything more than pass by the needs of our neighbours. Then we are unmerciful.

Jesus shows us this clearly in His parable about the "Good Samaritan". He calls the Samaritan compassionate, because he stopped when he saw someone in need and helped him. The others, who also saw his need, simply passed by and in that moment they became unmerciful. And yet their behaviour was almost understandable. Perhaps they were expected elsewhere; perhaps they had a ministry to perform. So they hastened to reach Jericho by evening, which was a day's journey away from Jerusalem. Perhaps it was shortly before nightfall. For the family's sake they could not endanger themselves. Worse things could have happened to them than to the one who lay there robbed and beaten. That is why they passed by him. They were probably not aware of the fact that this was a sin; after all, they did not cold-heartedly refuse to answer a call for help. They probably thought their obligation to get to Jericho quickly was more important than helping the robbed victim. If their conscience pricked them, they probably deceived themselves by saying that they did not have any opportunity to help in this case, because they did not have a donkey or a horse to carry the victim. So they passed him by, perhaps even a bit sad about his situation. But God had stamped them as "unmerciful".

Passing by someone who is in need! How often have we done this without realizing that God's words of judgment applied to us; "For judgment is without mercy to one who has shown no mercy" (Jas. 2: 13).

Perhaps we have never applied this terrible verdict to ourselves, because we have not realized that God was waiting for us to stop and be merciful to someone who was in need. But we passed by without taking advantage of the opportunity to help. We were unmerciful. What a shock it will be for us when we find ourselves at the judgment seat of God and hear Him pronounce the sentence of the unmerciful over us, "Depart from me, you cursed, into the eternal fire prepared for the devil and his angels" (Matt. 25: 41).

Who will be sentenced to eternal fire? Those who did not take in the strangers, care for the sick, visit the prisoners, feed the hungry—those who do not lovingly help their neighbours.

But Jesus has come so that we do not have to remain in sin and be damned with the world. He wants to remould us into His merciful image and let us come into His kingdom. Because Jesus loves us, He does not want us to be sent to hell because we were unmerciful. We must listen to His warning "Be alert!" Just because we have not rejected any requests, we cannot be sure that this judgment will not strike us! Every day we must entreat God to convict us of our sin of mercilessness in our daily life: "Show me, Lord, when I am about to pass by a person in need, either physically or otherwise. Let me see when my self-will is the reason, because I do not want others to frustrate my plans and intentions. Or show me where I do not have loving eyes for the needs of others, because I am so involved in my ego." Only those who ask will receive. Let us fight an intensive battle of prayer for mercifulness. Our fate in eternity depends upon this.

But this daily prayer is not enough. The good Samaritan not only had a merciful heart which could feel the needs of the other, but he was also willing to make a sacrifice for the needy. We have to commit ourselves to making sacrifices for our neighbour, for genuine mercy can only be practised when a sacrifice is included. The Samaritan sacrificed his safety; it could have cost him his life, to stay by the wounded man if the robbers had come back again. But we do not always have to risk our lives to be merciful. Sometimes it is just a very small thing that is expected from us, like giving money. Or perhaps, during times of scarcity, we ought to give others something to eat, something to wear or a place to sleep, even though we ourselves may have next to nothing. And how often does a small sacrifice of mercy simply mean giving others of our time? How often have we already become guilty in these matters?

Everything depends upon taking Jesus' exhortation seriously, "Be merciful!" I wonder, do we live according to the standards by which we will be judged by one day? "Be merciful, even as your Father is merciful" (Luke 6: 36). That means, for example, that we have to take the parable of the unmerciful servant seriously and apply it to our lives. The unmerciful servant was not merciful towards his fellow servant who was indebted to him. He did not see that since God was merciful to him and forgave him he was now bound to do the same. God is expecting us to be filled with mercy when others sin against us. He does not want us to keep account of their sin, but to forgive them mercifully.

Being unmerciful and not being able to forgive can one day cost us our lives and our inheritance in the kingdom of heaven. For Jesus says that the unmerciful servant, and all who follow his example, will be "delivered to the jailers", that means, they will be in Satan's kingdom. The Apostle Paul adds: "Those who do such things deserve to die" (Rom. 1: 31f). We deceive ourselves when we pretend that passing by others, or not being able to forgive, is something harmless. Jesus' words are true and we will be judged according to what He said. But by mercifulness we do not mean tolerating sin and no longer being willing in humble love to help others see their sin. If we neglect to do this, we will also become unmerciful, but in another sense, and this will also bring judgment down upon us.

If we repent of our lack of mercy and bring it under the blood of Jesus, we will also be compelled to go to those to whom we were unmerciful and seek to make amends by being especially loving and helpful towards them. Or if we can no longer reach them, we will bestow this kindness on others. Then the guilt of mercilessness will be blotted out in the blood of the Lamb for time and eternity.

So Jesus' words, "Be merciful, even as your Father is merciful", should not make us discouraged and despondent, when it seems as though our hard hearts, which continually pass by the needs of others, will never be made merciful. We must believe Jesus, when He says, "What is impossible with men is possible with God" (Luke 18: 27). With God everything is possible, for He is almighty. In Jesus there is redemption from all sins, even from mercilessness, for He has paid the full ransom price for our sins. We have been redeemed to be merciful. Whoever claims this in faith, ever anew, will find that he is changed into God's image of mercy, from one degree of glory to another and one day he will enter the Kingdom of God, the kingdom of love and mercy.

27. Mistrust

Mistrust is the opposite of trust. It is the root of disbelief towards God. We do not trust that His will, the motives behind His actions are always love. Such an attitude must provoke the wrath of God, who only has plans of love for His children. We can see this when we look at the Israelites in the desert. They mistrusted God and asserted that they would die, because He was leading them through the desert. This behaviour provoked the anger of God so much that He said, "How long will this people despise me? And how long will they not believe in me, in spite of all the signs which I have wrought among them?" (Num. 14: 11).

Mistrust means that we have a false picture of God in our hearts. We attribute evil intentions to God, because they are in our own hearts. When we mistrust God like this, we will find that He will treat us the same way that He treated the people of Israel in the desert. "As I live, says the Lord, what you have said in my hearing I will do to you: your dead bodies shall fall in this wilderness" (Num. 14: 28). God will let us experience what we have thought or said in mistrust, for instance, that God would forsake us, that the way He is leading us is difficult and no help will come. We will find that He deals with us just as we think He will. Whoever thinks that God's intentions are evil, will experience evil things. That is God's judgment upon our mistrust here on earth—and how great then will this judgment be in eternity!

Behind every mistrustful thought, even towards other people, there is something serious, namely an unspoken accusation. We think the other person does not have our best interests in mind; he does not want us to have anything good. This poison of mistrust spoils the relationship of trust to our heavenly Father and also to our neighbour. For if we mistrust the love and wisdom of God, we will unintentionally come into the same mistrustful, prejudiced attitude towards our fellow men and will become guilty towards them. This guilt, however, will accuse us before the judgment seat of God, if it is not brought into the light, repented of and forgiven through the blood of Jesus.

But if we are mistrustful towards our fellow men, we will be judged now in our everyday life. Because the relationship of trust is destroyed, we will no longer receive the love and the good things that they would otherwise have brought us. We become unhappy. This is the consequence of sin.

Mistrust separates us from God and man and poisons our whole life. For this reason we have to get rid of the sin of mistrust. But that is not the only reason. Our short lives on earth are a preparation for eternity. If we are mistrustful, how can we stand before God? We know that mistrust was one of the reasons why Adam and Eve were driven out of the Garden of Eden. They thought God wanted to withhold something good from them. This mistrust was fanned by Satan, the serpent. So man gave in to temptation and came under the dominion of the prince of this world. Mistrust brings us under the power of the old serpent, the enemy. The mistrustful place their trust in Satan instead of in God; they listen to his seductive voice.

This requires radical repentance. We cannot listen to this voice any more. It is the voice of the accuser, who wants to sow the poison of mistrust in our hearts or already has sown it. He suggests that God is withholding from us the best things. We have to hate our mistrust like the devil himself and begin to fight a battle to the point of shedding blood if we do not want to become the enemy's possession.

In the fight against mistrust we first have to be shown what the root of our mistrust against God and our neighbour is. It is ever-present concern for our ego. Will we get what we deserve? Will we be loved and respected enough? That is why we mistrust the leadings of God. That is why we suspect our neighbours. We think we are constantly in danger of getting a bad deal, or having others say negative things about us, or not receiving the love and respect we think we deserve. For this reason the mistrustful person imagines that while others appear to be friendly to him, they are in reality against him. He always supposes that others have ulterior motives. He even attributes evil to those who only want to do him good. And whenever there are misunderstandings, he immediately supposes that there is something bad. So he cannot be happy. Mistrust prevents bonds of love from being tied, for love believes all and does not think evil of his neighbours, even taking the risk of being disappointed.

Because egoism nourishes mistrust, it is very important, if we want to be freed from this, to make a serious sober commitment such as, "I do not want to be respected by certain people, I do not want to be popular. Lord, accept my commitment today. I do not want to worry about whether I get a bad deal; I do not want to be involved in myself. I want to trust that You will not let anything happen to me that would not be for my good. I always want to think the best of my neighbour and not give way to any mistrustful thoughts again . . ." Then we should go and seek ways to bring love and trust to those whom we have mistrusted. That will help us; for if we give others love, we will no longer centre around ourselves.

But we will still experience some defeats in our life of faith, because this poison of mistrust is so strong in our blood. It will not be easy to get rid of our mistrusting thoughts. Here there is only one medicine that will help: the blood of Jesus. We must claim it and count on the fact that His trusting love will flow into us. Jesus was constantly disappointed in His disciples, yet He continued to trust them until the very end. They had forsaken Him so disgracefully during His Passion, yet He trusted them again after His resurrection. He let them remain His disciples and even gave them new commissions. And for us He has gained the victory of this trusting love, although it cost Him so much. He wants to grant us this love which enables us to trust God and man.

Picture our heavenly Father. His love for His children was so unimaginably great that He not only gave away His beloved Son, but He even delivered His Son up to sinners, who mistreated Him cruelly, ridiculed Him and crucified Him like a criminal. All this to save us and make us happy. We must tell ourselves, "That is what my Father in heaven is like. He only has thoughts of love and peace for me, for He has proved His love." Therefore, we should be ashamed and ask for a deeper and deeper spirit of repentance, because we have wounded the loving heart of God so deeply through our mistrust. Renounce your mistrust, Satan and his evil works, because he only wants to bring you into misfortune both here and in eternity. Every time we begin to think mistrusting thoughts, we must say, "In the name of Jesus and through His redeeming blood depart from me, Satan, I will have nothing further to do with you and your seductive thoughts. I belong to Jesus, who has won for me a childlike trust in the Father's love."

If we go this way, we will be freed from the sin of mistrust, as surely as Jesus has redeemed us from all sin at Calvary.

28. Pleasing People: Conformity

"If I were still pleasing men, I should not be a servant of Christ" (Gal. 1: 10). With this statement, the Apostle Paul has touched upon a cancerous growth in life, especially among Christians. Because our human hearts are infected with sin, we seek the favour of our fellow men and not the favour of God. That is why it hurts us so much to lose the favour, love and recognition of men, especially of those whose favour is important to us. So we make every effort to please others. But then we are in danger of losing God's favour and Jesus will no longer look upon us as His servants and disciples.

This is an "either/or" situation. And it is especially important during this time of apostasy. If we are now seeking to please men, how quickly we could go over to the side of those who deny Jesus! In past years we have seen shocking examples of this among us Christians, and we have already seen something of the judgment such people reaped, who conformed because they were afraid.

In the face of all this the Lord is asking us, "What is the motive behind your talking, your behaviour?" Perhaps we are friendly towards strangers, but within our own family we are annoyed and grumpy. Our ulterior motive, although we may not be aware of it, is that we want the good opinion of strangers, their respect, their love and recognition, while we take this for granted in our own family. But if we were interested in God's favour and pleasure, we would be especially friendly at home, for God's sake. Another danger is that "when in Rome, we do as the Romans do". At work and elsewhere we conform to the people around us and do whatever they do, whether it involves gossiping with them, telling dirty jokes, accepting their opinions, conforming to their way of dress. All this because, as we say, we do not want to be "different".

Perhaps we even have other pretences: we do not want to offend people. If so we will not be able to tell them anything about our faith. But in reality we simply do not want to lose their favour. No matter what it costs, we want to avoid having any opponents. So we cater to men and do things we cannot justify. If we wanted to give a testimony of Jesus under these conditions, no one would believe us.

We are not at peace, but are tormented by our fear of others. We are afraid of what they may think of us. But how foolish this is! We are afraid of men and not afraid of God, who is really to be feared. Jesus says, "Do not fear those who kill the body but cannot kill the soul; rather fear him who can destroy both soul and body in hell" (Matt. 10: 28). Yes, we should be afraid of losing God's favour, by trying to gain the favour of man. For if God is no longer for us, we are lost, that is, God no longer uses His power for us and contends on our behalf. Yes, we are lost, if God's judgment is upon us. If we wish to please men, we cannot be His servants, neither here nor in eternity. He has power to deliver us up to Satan's kingdom. What good will recognition and favour from men do us, if we are separated from the Source of life, God Himself, and one day have to hear Him say, "You do not belong to Me!"?

No matter what it costs, our goal must be that we stand on God's side and that we have His good pleasure. Therefore, we must make a decision. We must denounce seeking to please people, so that we may obtain God's pleasure. Our fate for eternity depends upon this. Let us picture the baptism of Jesus and His transfiguration and listen to the Father's tender words of love, "This is my beloved Son, with whom I am well pleased" (Matt. 3: 17; 17: 5). Then we will sense that it is worth everything to receive God's commendation and will seek to please Him alone. Then we will partake fully of the love of God, which is actually our deepest longing. Moreover people cannot give us this much love and we will never be fully satisfied by them alone.

If we please God, He will love us and honour us, and

one day this will be manifested to all mankind. This is quite certain, whereas we can never be sure of getting love from people when we seek to please them. Tomorrow it may bring about our downfall. Human love is like dew, like a cloud that passes away. Perhaps the situation will change and tomorrow they will no longer be interested in taking care of us and being ready to help us. There is only one Person we can rely on; we can count on His love and all the gifts He has to give us. That is our LORD and GOD. What should we do, if God no longer counts us among His servants, if He is not for us? We cannot allow that to happen—in time or in eternity.

Jesus is exhorting us; "Choose Me; choose My way". In everything that we do and say we ought to please God. Let us make this commitment. It is a commitment to the cross, for it is painful when people withdraw their favour and we are no longer loved and respected by them. They may even reject us and be hostile to us. But then we will receive love from God and from those who are close to Him. That is always the case. The closer we are to the Lord and the more we seek to please Him, the more at one we are with those who are close to Him. Isn't that worth suffering for?

29. Pride: Haughtiness

"God opposes the proud" (1 Pet. 5: 5). This verse shows God's sharp verdict against the proud, for there can scarcely be anything worse than having God not only withdraw His grace from us but even flatly oppose us. Perhaps we complain that we are so spiritually dead, that we have difficulties praying, that God does not answer our prayers. This may be the reason. Because of our pride God opposes us and refuses to answer. Or perhaps we seem to be pursued by misfortune. We cannot succeed in anything we undertake no matter how hard we try. Why? God cannot bless us, because our pride has closed the door to Him.

The enemy tries to make every effort to keep us from recognizing this. For every time we do not bring our sin into the light and repent of it, he gets us in his hands. So in many cases he has covered up our pride. This hidden pride is the most dangerous sin. For instance, we cannot stand it, when people pay little attention to us and do not honour us, but pay honour to someone else. We cannot stand it, when we are not worth anything to others, because we do not have many talents or shining qualities or a charming personality. We cannot stand it, if someone reproaches us and humiliates us in the eyes of others. We cannot stand it, if we do not have a position of leadership and cannot set the pace. We do not realize that all of this stems from our pride.

On the contrary, we often feel sorry for ourselves, because people do not give us what our talents, education and capabilities deserve, or because we have to do work that is "beneath us". We feel sorry for ourselves, because we have not received the education or training necessary to carry out our job. Or we cannot bear the fact that our parents are uneducated, that we ourselves have not reached a prominent position. All these things oppress us and make us unhappy. We blame the external conditions, and we deceive ourselves about our real motives.

We cannot digest any criticism. We shut ourselves off from other people and may even think it is humility when we persist in this attitude, "I have to deal with this somehow myself". But in our hidden pride we are so mixed up that we cannot find the next step to ask for help and release. Our desire to have others think that we are especially humble and modest can also be hidden pride. We are too concerned about what others think of us. Pride can appear in many different forms. Only the Spirit of God can give us light about them.

Our hidden pride is like hidden poison, which threatens our spiritual life with death and will ruin everything in our lives. We have to make every effort to recognize our pride. By searching our consciences we have to let ourselves be shown the dangerous symptoms. We have to get to the bottom of this and ascertain which situation was difficult for us, because we were humiliated, embarrassed or overlooked.

Some Bible verses can help us get the proper attitude towards our pride:

'Every one who is arrogant is an abomination to the Lord . . ." (Prov. 16: 5).

"Pride goes before destruction, and a haughty spirit before a fall" (Prov. 16: 18).

"The Lord abundantly requites him who acts haughtily" (Ps. 31:23).

"What is exalted among men is an abomination in the sight of God" (Luke 16: 15).

It is a dreadful verdict that Jesus pronounces in the last verse over the proud and haughty. They are an abomination to God. That is why there will be dreadful judgment against the proud and lofty in the last days (Isa. 2: 12) and the Lord "Will put an end to the pride of the arrogant, and lay low the haughtiness of the ruthless" (Isa. 13: 11), when He comes again to judge mankind. The proud can await destruction. No matter how high the price, we have to experience redemption from our pride. Otherwise a terrible judgment will await us. We have to be horrified by our sin of pride, which is one of the most satanic sins, because Satan is pride personified. The proud belong to his kingdom. Through their pride they are tilling the ground for many other sins. If we are not determined to make a radical break with our pride and to strive for humility, we will never be free from Satan's nets.

The Word of God gives us clear directives. First, "Humble yourselves therefore under the mighty hand of God" (1 Pet. 5: 6). In practical life it can look like this: If we are denied an honour, an office, a position of leadership, something that our pride has been striving for, we must humble ourselves beneath the mighty hand of God. We must surrender our will to God; we must yield to everything that humiliates us. We must say, "Yes, Father", to the flaws in our personality, to our insufficient education and talents, to our family situation, to being a sinner again and again, to our own faults reflected in the behaviour of our children, etc. Let us say, "I thank You, Father, for taking pains with me and thinking up this way of humiliation for me so that I can be freed from my pride." If we call to the Lord in this way, we will find that God will answer this prayer.

Then the second thing that Jesus advises us to do: We should humble ourselves as Jesus did, the Son of God, the Lord Most High, at whose feet the angels fall, bringing Him homage. It is written; "Taking the form of a servant . . . he humbled himself" (Phil. 2: 7, 8). Now He is calling to us sinful men, who actually deserve nothing more than the place of lowliness, "Whoever humbles himself will be exalted" (Matt. 23: 12). Let us respond to Jesus' challenge by voluntarily humbling ourselves. That will help us to become humble, for when we go Jesus' way of lowliness, some of our pride will crumble. Let us choose freely a lowly position that will humble us. Whenever possible, we should not accept any titles or honours; we should not try to stand out in any group, or strive for positions of honour. On the contrary, let us take advantage of the opportunities to step back and let others receive the honour that we may deserve. Let us be quiet when we have the opportunity to draw attention to ourselves.

Above all, let us admit our mistakes and sins to a counsellor, or to others when it is necessary, because that often humiliates us the most. Only true humiliations can really make us humble and free us from pride. Whoever becomes a "friend" of humiliations will find that they have great power. When they are accepted in love for Jesus, they are like a hammer that smashes our pride to pieces.

But it is also necessary to wage an intensive battle of faith against the sinful power of pride, behind which Satan stands, in order to be freed from it. We must act according to the advice of the Holy Scriptures and accept humiliations, but at the same time bring the bondage of pride daily under the blood of the Lamb, who has released us from this spirit of pride. We have to fight a battle of faith against "principalities and powers" without becoming tired and discouraged. We must fight in the knowledge that Jesus will be victorious, for He was victorious on the cross and redeemed us to humility. Then we will experience the fulfilment of God's promise to come and dwell with the humble (Isa. 57: 15).

Jesus could say that He was "lowly in heart" (Matt. 11: 29). What radiance there is in the life of a truly humble person: the majesty of Jesus Christ shone forth in Him, the humble and lowly Lord, on His bitter way to Calvary. Could it be that He who was "lowly in heart" would not do everything possible to clothe His disciples with this virtue also? He has the power to make us humble men who bear His radiance and majesty. For this He offered His sacrifice on Calvary. On the cross He trod the head of the serpent under His feet—the serpent who personifies pride. He is Victor over sin and the power of pride. If we call upon the Lamb of God, who overcame our pride, He will make us overcomers too.

30. Quarrelsomeness: Dissension

In Gal. 5:19-21 the Apostle Paul lists the sins which he calls "works of the flesh" and tells us very pointedly, "... I warn you, as I warned you before, that those who do such things shall not inherit the kingdom of God" (v. 21). They are sins like immorality, drunkenness, licentiousness and others, which are known to us as vices.

But in this list there is also a sin that we seldom think will prevent us from inheriting the kingdom of God. Dissension—disrupting peaceful relationships with quarrelsomeness. Yes, the Holy Scriptures take this sin so seriously that the Apostle Paul uses four different expressions to describe it, because it will exclude us from the Kingdom of God: enmity, strife, dissension, party spirit.

A mighty warning from God, which we usually manage to miss. If we took it seriously, the Church of God would not be split up into so many factions and there would not be so many quarrels. There was no request more urgent to Jesus' heart than that His own be at one among each other. That was His last plea. The fact that scarcely anyone listens to this plea shows that Jesus is not the Lord in His Church; we do not take it for granted that His commandments are binding for us. It shows that His Church, and we as His members, often live apart from Him; we lead a life of sin, of quarrelling, of enmity, etc. As the Body of Christ we are disfiguring the Head, Jesus Christ, and discrediting Him and His teaching of love. So we become guilty towards countless people who therefore take offence at Christianity. But at the same time, without actually being aware of it, we have become separated from Jesus, the Head, and live under the domination of him who incites all enmity, hatred, strife and dissension. Yes, we destroy the Kingdom of God, which is built up by the unity of love, but which is torn apart by strife and disunity.

There are not enough words to express what serious consequences strife and enmity always have in families, churches and other groups within His Church. The Holy Scriptures say that everything in our lives is written down in a book of remembrance (Mal. 3: 16), so our debts with respect to these sins will usually be large. For what have we done to prevent such quarrels and divisions? We are supposed to be Jesus' peacemakers, but instead we have often helped to fan the flames of enmity. One day God will ask us whether we have helped to attain peace through kind and loving words in families, in Christian fellowships and works, or whether we have yielded to quarrelsomeness or were even the initiator of quarrels.

The tendency to fan the flames, whenever there is a slight bit of tension, sits deeply in all our hearts. And the tiny spark of a disparaging remark, which we may throw into a conversation, can become a blazing fire in churches, fellowships or families. One day when we stand before the judgment seat of God, the judgment for all the terrible things that such quarrelling and division may have done to the Kingdom of God will fall upon us.

The Holy Scriptures place much emphasis upon this sin, mentioning it four times within one verse, warning us that it can exclude us from the Kingdom of God. Therefore we must react accordingly by taking this sin specially seriously and not tolerating it any more in our lives. But we will only fight against it with all seriousness, if we first call it clearly by name, as the Holy Scriptures do. We must not embellish it by piously pretending to be defending the truth or by saying it is merely "unavoidable family problems", etc. We have to get rid of such excuses. Usually our desire to maintain truth and justice, even theologically, is not pure. We can apply the words that the Apostle Paul wrote to the Corinthians about their pious divisions (Pauline, Apolline . . .), "While there is jealousy and strife among you, are you not of the flesh, and behaving like ordinary men?" (1 Cor. 3: 3).

Quarrelling and dissension always have to do with our "flesh". The root is pride together with envy, jealousy and other sins. The proud think that their opinion alone is right. They cannot see the good points of others, as the humble do, and appreciate their opinions. That is why there is such disagreement, strife and quarrelling and even irreconciliation in families and in other groups.

The Holy Scriptures are not interested in whether we are right or wrong when there is a problem in our family or in our church. Rather they clearly state: Whenever we quarrel with others, we belong to those who will not inherit the Kingdom of God, if we do not stretch out our hand to our opponent and answer the wrong he has done us with forgiving, long-suffering love (Matt. 5: 23 ff). In this matter God is relentless in His demands and He has a right to be. For when we were His enemies, He forgave us everything in Jesus. We continually cause Him trouble with our sins, much more trouble than any person could cause us, and He still continues to bear with us. He loves us and responds to the sorrow that we cause Him with love and bestows good gifts upon us lavishly.

That is why there is nothing that provokes the wrath of God against us more than when we fight against others instead of being kind to them, and covering up their mistakes as He does with ours. Then the terrible punishment of God will strike us. He will shut us out of His kingdom, even though we could have shared in it through Jesus' forgiveness. Then we will have to go to the kingdom where all those who lived in hatred, envy, lies and quarrels here on earth will dwell. Therefore, let us open our eyes to see what kind of seeds we are sowing through our quarrelsomeness.

We have to get rid of our tendency to fight—no matter whether it is in the realm of inheritance, marriage or law or whether it is in the realm of spiritual teachings and doctrines. What could help us more than looking at the picture of Jesus ever anew? He was the Prince of peace, the Peacemaker, who did not revile in return when He was reviled, who did not threaten when He suffered, but trusted Him who judges justly (1 Pet. 2: 23). He reacted like a lamb, heaping burning coals of love upon the heads of those who tortured Him to death. He wants to call us to follow Him on His way. If we are on His way, we will belong to Him here and in eternity. Then Satan will not have any claim on us.

Let the words of Scripture be binding for us: "Do not be overcome by evil, but overcome evil with good" (Rom. 12: 21). Let us take the first step, go to our brother and be reconciled with him when it is a personal matter, or stretch out the hand of love to a brother in a different Christian camp under the cross of Christ, respecting his opinions, commissions and leadings even if they should be different from ours. If we do not do this, we will lose the Kingdom of God in spite of all the supposed efforts we make on its behalf. For those who quarrel and demand their rights will never inherit the Kingdom of God.

Therefore, we must entreat Jesus, "Let me see my secret sin of quarrelsomeness, fighting and dissension", and He will answer and show us our sin. Then we will no longer be able to thrust the sword into others, but only into ourselves. Jesus has come as Love eternal and has, on the cross, won the victory over strife. He will be victorious in us also, if we want to be set free from this sin. This victory is valid for all of us who are quarrelsome; it is valid for everyone who claims it in faith.

31. Rebellion

Rebellion was the sin of the followers of Korah (Num. 16), of those who murmured and protested against their leaders and against those who had special privileges and blessings that they themselves did not have. This rebellious spirit can be especially found among the pious. God punished the children of Korah in the most severe way possible. They had to pay for their rebellious spirit with death. A rebellious spirit contains the poison of the devil, for Satan is the chief of rebels. Because Satan did not have the same position as God, he rebelled against Him. We can see that the spirit of rebellion is born out of envy and pride. Satan makes every effort to pour this poison into the hearts of believers and to get them into his hands. It is a destructive force, just as humble, serving love is a constructive force. Loving builds the kingdom of love, but the spirit of rebellion builds hell. Every rebellious spirit of criticism, of protest against arrangements made by our superiors, adds bricks to the building of the kingdom of hell.

But the uncanny thing about rebellion is that it is often camouflaged and for this reason many are affected by it. It is so contagious. Today we can see this on a large scale. It comes with smart arguments and ideas of reform, which seemingly seek to improve poor conditions, and pretend to give the oppressed a more human life, more freedom and so on. These good intentions are supposed to justify the use of violence against the established order, to destroy all authorities, then seek to do away with all rules and with God's commandments. What leads to violence and chaos on a large scale begins in our small sphere of life with similar satanic camouflage. "Could God really have meant that? Could He really have meant that I should be the one to be subject to others, to obey others and their rules? I have been created with a free will and do not need to be subject to anyone."

Usually we try to make such reactions seem harmless and do not realize that "rebellion is as the sin of witchcraft" (1 Sam. 15: 23). Satan, the rebel, has poured this poison into our thought world. He knows that this will bring the death sentence upon us as it did for the company of Korah, that is, we could come into the hands of the prince of hell and deserve to die the "second death", (Rev. 20: 14, 15; 21: 8) a dreadful, continual dying. But even here in this life dreadful judgment will come upon the rebels. We can see this in our times. Those who rebel die in their souls; their lives become empty and meaningless. An increasing suicide rate is the consequence. For rebels are condemned to death.

If we do not want to be servants of Satan, we must take a clear stand against every spirit of rebellion in us. The first step is to surrender our own opinions completely to God. We must make every effort to adjust to the established order into which God has placed us and commit ourselves to recognizing authorities and their decisions. As a sign of our willingness, we should approach our superiors, no matter who they may be—yes, even the overbearing (1 Pet. 2: 18)—with respect and obedience. However, if we should see something that needs to be changed, we should ask them humbly to do this and at the same time lay this concern before God, who can move people's hearts.

But the important thing, if we do not want to come into the grip of Satan, the chief of the rebels, is that we call upon the name of Jesus as soon as rebellious thoughts begin to arise in us. Jesus, the Son of God, humbly subjected Himself to people, like His parents in Nazareth, ". . . and was obedient to them" (Luke 2:51). Even in the darkest hours, when everything seemed to be meaningless, He did not rebel against the incomprehensible leadings of God, but rather He trusted the Father. Through His obedience He has also redeemed us from the spirit of rebellion. We must say that over and over again and pray:

Let praises ring aloud this day,

That by this mighty name
The powers of hell are put to flight
and made to tremble!
W.J. 186

In the name of Jesus there is great power. Yes, before it hell trembles and its attacks will yield, for the name of Jesus is a victorious name. In it is victory over every power of sin. Therefore, we can claim God's promise, "Everyone who calls upon the name of the Lord will be saved" (Rom. 10: 13).

If we enter the battle of faith against the spirit of rebellion with complete resolution, then Jesus, who has paid for our satanic rebellion with His death, will set us free.

32. Repression: Suppression

Now and then we may find that we suddenly become depressed without actually knowing why. Others around us say, "You are so sullen today. What's the matter?"

Usually we have not been able to cope with an unpleasant experience and we have repressed it into our subconscious. But everything that is in our subconscious, that we are not aware of, that we do not want to confront, is in darkness. And Satan has power over this darkness. He is the lord in the kingdom of darkness, and if we come under his power we too will be in darkness.

Perhaps there are two doctors in a town. One has only a few patients, the other has more than he can handle. Every time the first one hears how much the other has to do, he becomes depressed and sullen. His whole family suffers from this. A friend who watches carefully can immediately understand what has happened; "He cannot cope with this humiliation." But strangely enough, the one who has to suffer the humiliation is often unaware of the reason behind his bad temper. He persuades himself that he has to handle all the difficult cases, the ones that require more time and more knowledge. So in this way he does not see the root of his grumpiness and his unfriendliness towards his colleague.

Or perhaps two young girls are sitting together. A young man comes in and one of them has to stand by and watch him talk to her friend and not pay the slightest attention to her. Later at home her mother is amazed how sullen her daughter is, how nasty she can be. Everything is too much for her; she is not willing to do anything. The root lies in this experience. She cannot accept the fact that she is not as popular as her friend.

We—just like this doctor and young girl—usually tend to suppress our humiliations, for instance being overlooked by others. As a result we can never begin to fight against our pride and desire for attention that these experiences bring to the fore. We do not want to confront the situation by saying to ourselves, "I am so depressed and bad-tempered, rebelling against others, perhaps with mean and angry words, because I could not cope with this humiliation. I am proud, jealous, envious. That is why I cannot cope with this situation." If we would admit this, we could find help. Then we could begin to fight against pride and envy. Then we could enter a battle of prayer and faith, ask for hatred towards this sin of pride and then claim the blood of the Lamb, that will set us free.

But that is not possible as long as we continue to suppress things, because we do not want to bring the sin of pride into the light. Ultimately we do not want God to begin to work on this sin, judging us and chastening us. But this "hidden pride" is a most dangerous thing for our spiritual and emotional life. We cannot afford to have this pride. If we repress something unpleasant or difficult, we will have to bear the consequences. This pride takes such a high toll that many people, especially Christians, become depressed and melancholy and even have to be committed to mental institutions. If you do research in this matter, you will find that eighty per cent of depressive and melancholic cases are caused by this hidden pride, which people have always suppressed into their subconscious and never brought into the light.

So such Christians, who do not want to confront and admit their desire for attention, their pride and envy, will harvest misfortune, despair and even mental illness here on earth. But if the consequences of not wanting to admit our sin are so great here on earth, how much greater must they be in eternity! What severe judgment must be awaiting Christians with their hidden pride! So here we have to bring our sin into the light, if we do not want the light of God's holy fire to expose and judge us in the other world.

Thus we have to admit that we sell ourselves to Satan whenever our pride cannot bear playing second fiddle to someone else and we do not bring this pride into the light. But if we admit the truth, it will make us free. Then Jesus

Christ, the Light, will be present. And He will bring peace and joy into our hearts and redeem us from the serious outcome of our sin. He will preserve us from melancholy and mental illness.

This is an "either/or" situation. Either we suppress things and wind up with shattered lives, perhaps even in mental institutions," or we will admit our sin of pride and envy and end in light and joy. Then our lives will be filled with power and our activities will be a blessing for others; instead of being melancholy, we will be radiant with the joy of Jesus. Because it is an "either/or" situation, whose consequences reach into eternity, it means bringing everything into the light that we would rather repress.

The first step towards redemption is to find out why we are so sullen. We should think of everything we have experienced recently and how we reacted. And then we must break our pact with the sins of pride or envy by not suppressing them, but admitting and unmasking them, confessing them to a counsellor or to someone else, if it will humiliate us. Next we must call on Jesus Christ to let His blood free us. If we bring Him our pride, being willing to have Him chasten and humble us, then we will be transformed. Then we will experience release. Then we will no longer be sullen and mean, no longer in despair, nor emotionally ill. Humiliations are always painful for us, but they will become easy when we begin to give thanks for them. God is doing us a great service through His work of chastening; He is redeeming us from our hidden pride, which ruins our lives and makes us unhappy. He yearns to give us joyful and fulfilled lives.

Not until I find my sin unbearable and begin to hate it, will I use the scalpel to remove my cancerous growth of sin. Not until then will something new begin to blossom in my life.

33. Ridicule: Scoffing

How quickly we try to dispose of scoffing and ridicule as something funny and harmless. Yet we have to admit that ridicule is a sin, although this sin, in contrast to many others, even has a good appearance sometimes. At parties and other get-togethers ridicule can create a "humorous" atmosphere; it does not cost us anything; it makes people laugh and wins us friends.

But the spirit of ridicule (which is not to be mistaken for the divine gift of humour) is a spirit from the devil. That we can see when we think of how Jesus was crowned with the crown of thorns. Here hell was let loose; it raged against its Creator. Ridicule, which often hurts so deeply, stems from hell. And whatever comes from hell and is sown by us will make us reap the punishment of hell. So if we tend to ridicule much, we have to see clearly that it is a serious sin, which will bring us judgment. The second letter of Peter lists the "scoffer" as one of the types of antichristian men that will appear in the last times (2 Pet. 3: 3).

The Holy Scriptures also tell us more about the wickedness of scoffing. "The scoffer is an abomination to men" (Prov. 24: 9b). The first Psalm begins "Blessed is the man who walks not in the counsel of the wicked ... nor sits in the seat of scoffers" (Ps. 1: 1). In Proverbs 21: 24 it is written, " 'Scoffer' is the name of the proud, haughty man who acts with arrogant pride." Scoffing and ridicule have one root: pride.

Curses, insults and scorn coming out of the mouths of the proud is like poison from hell—just as blessing and humble love for one another is what makes heaven heaven. And whoever wants to enter heavenly glory has to be set free from this poison of ridicule at all costs.

So that we can see this sin and its cause more clearly, and fight against it better, we have to realize how wicked our pride is when it is at work in this sin.

Why did the adherents of the Pharisees ridicule Jesus? Because they rebelled against having the Son of God as their Lord. They lacked true power to fight against Him and so they fought with ridicule, mockery and abuse. Because they really did not have any way to attack the Holy One of God, they sought to humiliate Him with ridicule.

We do the same thing, when we envy certain people, are bitter towards them or when we hate them. We rebel against them by using cheap and dirty tactics, against which no one can defend himself. We heap ridicule upon them. Yes, only a small, spiteful remark, a small bit of irony about a third person can ruin his reputation. And we know that our reputation is often worth more to us than our lives. So we have to realize that we can almost kill a person through mockery, ridicule or irony.

One day we will find out how much damage we have caused. We will have to see the wounds that our ridicule brought others and the scars that they had to bear for life. Ridicule and scoffing are devilish and are the sign of the people inspired by Satan in the last times. If we persist in ridiculing others, we will fall into Satan's hands and judgment will catch up with us in the other world.

No matter what the cost, we must be set free from scoffing. But how? The first important thing to do is to let ourselves be shown, by the light of God, that these mean, underhanded and dirty tactics come from hell—even if the enemy seeks to make this sin seem harmless. Furthermore, it will help us if we meditate much upon Jesus, crowned with the crown of thorns. Then, instead of scoffing, we will be filled with deep shame over what we have done to the King of kings through ridicule. Whoever continues to live in this sin without hating it and fighting a battle of faith against it will join the ranks of the opponents of Jesus.

In every specific case we must ask for the Spirit of truth so that we can see why we react so quickly towards certain people with ironic remarks. Then we will see the evil root in our hearts; perhaps envy, jealousy or bitterness. Our irony is often the weapon of revenge, which we use maliciously, because we are too cowardly to tell the other person something to his face or to speak openly with him.

But listen to what Scripture says: "Repent!"—about our envy, our bitterness, or whatever the root might be, and the godly sorrow we ask for will drive us into the arms of Jesus. Jesus will rescue us from this sin, which binds us to Satan, for Jesus has come to "destroy the works of the devil" (1 John 3: 8) and to establish the kingdom of love where there will not be any ridicule or scoffing. Jesus is standing before us as the Lord crowned with the crown of thorns, as the Lamb of God. A lamb does not ridicule, but it is ridiculed. We have been redeemed to bear the image of the Lamb. As the followers of Jesus we should be prepared to be laden with ridicule, mockery and disgrace for His name's sake; for "a servant is not greater than his master" (John 13: 16). Then we will lose our desire to ridicule and, instead, we will learn how to bless our enemies.

Behind this sin is Satan and he is ready to fight. Are we ready too? Then Jesus will be on our side and He is always the Victor.

34. Selfishness: Stinginess

Selfishness, stinginess is an especially serious sin. The Bible implies this when it says, "The love of money is the root of all evils" (1 Tim. 6: 10). It is clear that all who have an exaggerated love of earthly things will be excluded from the Kingdom of God, for it is written that they will not "inherit the kingdom of God" (1 Cor. 6: 10 and see Eph. 5: 5). Yes, selfishness, like covetousness, is idolatry. "On account of these the wrath of God is coming upon the sons of disobedience" (Col. 3: 5b, 6).

Because the selfish have such a serious punishment awaiting them, and the wrath of God is upon them now, we have to become free from stinginess at all costs. It is more or less in all people, even if it is not so obvious in some. It can appear with seemingly harmless symptoms. "Thriftiness", or "smart planning" can be possible camouflages.

Selfishness reveals its true face when it is hard for us to give away something. That can happen in many areas, depending upon what our heart is especially attached to. So a stingy person will sometimes "wallow" in his possessions, not wanting to give them away, until he almost drowns in them. Often he refuses to give to those who ask, and he will never part with any money or possessions voluntarily. He is bound to the transient things of this earth. But he does not realize that he is also bound to the prince of this world, to Satan. He has become his servant here and one day will not inherit the Kingdom of God, even if he did seem to believe in Jesus on earth.

We Christians often pretend that we are not stingy, yet we are bound to our possessions. How often we saw this in my country, Germany, when people were asked to take in refugees and homeless during and after the Second World War. People tried to convince themselves that they were obliged to keep home, furniture and other things intact for the sake of their own children. They thought, out of love for their children, they could not possibly do anything but refuse to take in the homeless and the refugees, or at the most, give them the worst room and the poorest goods. Even Christians did not realize that they were being stingy and were sinning against their neighbour who was in need.

As long as we are not confronted by such extraordinary situations, we have to take advantage of the time to overcome this sin. For selfishness is the opposite of love, which gives away everything, and makes us and others happy by doing so. Stinginess makes us trespass against love, which is a characteristic of the divine and can make life on earth paradise. The selfish are sowing terrible seeds during their short life on earth, which will sprout in the other world. Their inheritance will be the kingdom of darkness, where God's wrath will be wrought upon them.

Therefore, let us declare war on the selfishness in our hearts! Jesus warns us so urgently, "Watch, and be on your guard against avarice of any kind, for a man's life is not made secure by what he owns" (Luke 12: 15 Jerusalem Bible). At the same time, Jesus reveals to us the main root of stinginess. We are blind and cannot see what the real treasure is, the "treasure in heaven", God Himself. If God is the great love of our lives, then we are "rich in Him" and will not be attached to the riches of this world. Then we will receive everything from Him that we need for this life. However, if God is not the "treasure" of our lives, if we seek earthly, transient things, we will be captivated by them and become a slave of stinginess and Satan. We will submit to stinginess every time, if we do not truly love Jesus and are not completely committed to Him. He not only gives us everlasting, eternal treasures, but will also give us abundantly everything we need for our life here, if we will only let go and give things up for His sake.

The way to get rid of this destructive stinginess is to "let go"! Jesus Himself has given us this advice, "Freely you have received, freely give" (Matt. 10: 8). But who can do this? Only those who have found complete abundance in Jesus and at the same time in faith count on His promise, "Give, and it will be given to you; good measure, pressed down, shaken together, running over" (Luke 6: 38). We must dare to let go and give away what we would rather cling to. And if we take this step in love for Jesus, we will experience that He will act according to His promise and give us a hundredfold in return. Such experiences will encourage us to continue to give up things. Jesus has redeemed us from the futile ways inherited from our fathers (1 Pet. 1: 18) and has transplanted us into His kingdom where love reigns.

35. Self-Pity

Everything that is an enemy of love is sin. Indeed, the sin against love is the greatest sin, because love is the greatest achievement of Jesus' redemption.

Self-pity is one of the sins against love. Having compassion for others is an attribute of love. But when we pity ourselves, we only love ourselves, not others. Our love is on the wrong track; it has a false object. Although our love should really belong to our neighbours, we withdraw it from them and become guilty of withholding love from them. Self-pity belongs to the "ego-illnesses". We pamper our egos, in which this sin sits; yet this sin will have to die if the new man is to arise.

This is especially evident during times when God chastens and judges us. During such times we often pity ourselves. It is especially dangerous, because we usually do not recognize it as a sin and do not realize that our self-pity strengthens our "old man". It places us in the enemy's hand and deprives us of the possibility of overcoming in our fight against sin.

The root of self-pity is our reluctance to admit that we are sinners, who need to be chastened. If we recognized our sins and mistakes, we would be grateful when God begins to attack them, when He judges and chastens us, even though it might hurt. Instead of pitying ourselves and complaining, we would only find that what we have to suffer in the way of chastening is much too little.

Those who pity themselves do not have the right attitude towards sin. Although they do not realize it, they cannot admit their sin. When they get into trouble, they accuse God instead of themselves and thus they set up a barrier against God, they even call down His wrath upon themselves and forfeit their heavenly glory. Those who pity themselves do not act according to the words of Scripture, "Strive ... for the holiness without which no one will see the Lord" (Heb. 12: 14).

They are not consumed by the desire to attain holiness and see Jesus. Rather, they are fascinated by their own egos. When they are being chastened and judged by God, they complain that things are not going well with them. That makes them incapable of seeing that it is the chastening that will help them "share his holiness" (Heb. 12: 10). Nor can they see that Satan is standing behind them, laughing scornfully when they complain and pity themselves. For now he has attained his goal, they have fallen prey to an idol, their own egos. Satan knows that self-pity furthers every other sin and therefore it is a triumph for him.

Yes, with our self-pity we are reacting just the opposite of how the Holy Scriptures say we should act. We should judge ourselves. That means that we are supposed to judge ourselves especially severely when God judges and chastens us. The Apostle Paul writes, "But if we judged ourselves truly, we should not be judged. But when we are judged by the Lord, we are chastened so that we may not be condemned along with the world" (1 Cor. 11:31,32).

The Holy Scriptures are challenging us to take a stand against our "old man", to condemn it with its sin so that God does not have to do this one day. "It is a fearful thing to fall into the hands of the living God" (Heb. 10: 31), for God, the Judge, is a consuming Fire. That is why our goal must always be to let ourselves be judged for our egoistic sins like self-pity. We must condemn ourselves so that the judgment of God, His severe punishment, will not strike us in eternity.

We must renounce our self-pity with complete resoluteness. We cannot afford to give any room in our hearts to self-pity, which nourishes many other sins.

At the very first thought of self-pity that comes to us, we must call upon the blood of the Lamb and say aloud, or to ourselves:

> I do not want to have anything more to do with self-pity; I am a sinner and need this judgment and chastening. I am receiving a lenient punishment for what my deeds are really worth.

For the sake of Your redemption, Jesus, I will not let You go unless You change my self-pity into compassion for others. I want to condemn my self-pity ever anew, so that You will not have to judge me for it one day.

Then Jesus will have compassion on us; then He will finish His work of education in us and take us out of this school again at His timing. When we take measures against our self-pity without sparing ourselves, God the Father will spare us and lovingly treat us like His own Son.

Self-pity and making excuses are the soil that nourishes our sin. Whoever wants to be set free from his sin must pull it out of this soil no matter how high the price.

36. Self-Righteousness: Self-Justification

The self-righteous proclaim that they are righteous and that everything they say and do is right. There is one thing they cannot bear to hear: others questioning whether their behaviour was right. That is why they rebel and defend themselves, usually by adding that others do not understand them and do them wrong. They immediately turn the point of the sword around, by accusing others and keeping them from telling them the truth about themselves. The self-righteous put on a suit of armour so that no criticism can ever hit them. The self-righteous do not think it is necessary to fight against sin, since they are perfect. And so they will never make any inroads in any areas of their sinful disposition. On the contrary, all the other sins are nourished; they can grow and flourish. That is the terrible result of a life of self-righteousness. Man remains a slave to his sins and is separated from Jesus, no matter how pious he may appear to be, for he is living in a lie and is clinging to it. However, only truth, if we listen to it and accept it, can set us free. When the self-righteous reject the truth, they are rejecting Jesus, who is Truth.

If in our self-righteousness, we have rejected the warning voice of God, the voice of truth, even when it has come through another person, it is questionable whether the warning will come to us again. We have chased it away. But one day it will reach us—the day when we appear before the judgment seat of Christ. Then there will be a terrible judgment of those who were "hardened", who did not want to accept God's voice, His warnings, admonitions and judgments, even through other people. Because sin spreads, we will reap an evil harvest in eternity. Then it will be too late to repent.

Self-righteousness is probably the most serious sin; it is the root of all other sins, and they cannot be broken as long as we have not begun to fight against this sinful root. This sin is the root of the hot-tempered, who lash out immediately; of the irritated, who always have to have the last word; of the inhibited, who cannot move about freely, because they do not want to do anything wrong; of the silent, who do not say anything, because they do not want to say anything wrong; of the depressed, who cannot bear to be the way they are or to act the way they do; of the bitter, because they cannot admit that they are the ones who caused their bitter situation through their own sin. Self-righteousness has its effects in every sinful disposition.

In addition self-righteousness is one of the main sins that nailed Jesus to the cross. People did not want to hear His message, "Repent!", because they did not want to admit that as sinful men they needed a Saviour. Therefore, they cried out, "Crucify Him". If we do not hate this sin above all other sins and fight a battle to the point of shedding blood, we will be lost. Then the door to Jesus' kingdom of truth will be closed to us. For the self-righteous, who do not want to hear the truth about themselves and who often become untruthful when they defend themselves, are living in a lie and therefore they belong to Satan, who was a liar from the very beginning. But who realizes that his self-righteousness has made him a slave to Satan and a member of his kingdom? As a Christian he is perhaps convinced that he is a disciple of Jesus and belongs to His kingdom. But Jesus speaks these very hard words to the self-righteous, "You are those who justify yourselves before men, but God knows your hearts; for what is exalted among men (because, according to their own statements, everything is all right) is an abomination in the sight of God" (Luke 16: 15).

How terrible these words are which Jesus says to the self-righteous! God abhors them, or, in other words, on the day of judgment God will hurl them into darkness. Why? Because the self-righteous are so proud and are not prepared to admit that anything in their words and actions is not right. It would humiliate them to do that. Only the humble could do it. The proud and self-righteous, who pretend that they are blameless, are called hypocrites by Jesus, just like the Pharisees, because they live a lie. The Lord hurls this terrible question at them, "How are you to escape being sentenced to hell?" (Matt. 23: 33).

We have to be redeemed from our self-righteousness no matter what the cost. We have to make every effort to be freed from bondage. The first step (which hypocrites also have to take, since hypocrisy and self-righteousness usually belong together) is to ask for light. For the self-righteous must hear Jesus saying to them, "Now that you say, 'We see', your guilt remains" (John 9: 41). The self-righteous are blind about themselves; they do not want to see their sins.

If someone says to us, "You are so self-righteous", and we cannot accept it, we have to cry to God daily, "Send Your light and Your truth—Reveal everything that is not pure in Your light—Place my unknown sins in the light of Your countenance." And God who has promised to answer such prayers, because they are according to His will, will give us light. For Jesus has come to give sight to the blind, as it is written in Luke 4: 18. If He has given sight to the physically blind, how much more will He prove His might to give sight to our souls for our sins. His love wants to do this. He is Light and Truth and wants to send us His Spirit of truth. He has redeemed us so that we could become children of light and recognize the truth about ourselves, which will make us free (John 8: 32). We will certainly discover this, if we earnestly beg for light.

Let us offer this prayer:
Let me open my heart and listen to others when people say the truth about me. I want to accept this practical help to be freed from the curse of blind self-righteousness. It is so hard for me to hear others tell me about my weaknesses and my mistakes. But I want to accept it as Your special offer of love to me, because Your warning voice comes to me through such people. I want to give thanks for every person

who calls my attention to my mistakes. And when this does not happen, I want to ask the people around me to tell me everything. And even if the admonitions and accusations are not one hundred per cent true, I want to use the opportunity to break my self-righteousness and self-justification. I want to fight to the point of shedding blood.

Blind pride goes hand in hand with self-righteousness, and this co-sin usually has to be cleansed through chastening. Through chastening we are to gain sight for our real condition. Then we will learn that we are really sinners and how greatly we fall short of the glory of God (Rev. 3: 18 f.). Chastening makes the proud humble, *if* we accept it. Yes, if the chastening shows us the truth about ourselves and helps us repent, we will be helped. But whoever bears it full of self-pity with such pious expressions as "I want to take it from God's hand" will never be redeemed from the dreadful sin of self-righteousness. Chastenings, such as sickness, working with difficult people, frustration of one's own wishes and plans, humiliations and disappointments of all sorts, are to serve to bring our sins into the light and help us recognize them. Then we can only beat our own breasts and say, "We are receiving the due reward of our deeds" (Luke 23: 41). When we are humiliated in this way, our proud self-righteousness will be healed. We will have gained our sight.

Yet all these things could not help us, if there were not Someone, who was able to be silent, when people accused Him unjustly: Jesus, the Lamb of God, who was "dumb before His shearers". He has also redeemed us to be silent so that we no longer have to justify ourselves in words or thoughts. Jesus has conquered the enemy, the old liar, and set us free from all self-justification. He is the Saviour, who will also heal this sinful ailment, as it is written, "With his stripes we are healed" (Isa. 53: 5).

He will even heal the worst type of self-righteousness: thinking that we are not self-righteous at all. His blood will cleanse us in a long healing process, whose first sign of progress is that we will be able to admit our self-righteousness. "That's the way I am, full of self-righteous pride." If we confess our sins and repent of them, He will cleanse us from all unrighteousness (1 John 1: 9). Every self-righteous thought loses its power, as soon as we bring it under the blood of Jesus. Therefore, we must be alert. If we cannot understand an accusation or a reproach, there is still one way open to us—we can ask God to give us the true perspectives through His Spirit. Then we will see clearly how we caused the situation. In times of quiet prayer God will show us our "Account Book". Certainly once in a while there may be a mistake that has to be explained. But then we must pray about it so that we can explain it humbly.

Let us persevere in the battle of faith, claiming the victory of Jesus ever anew, prepared to accept God's chastening. We will find that the chains of self-righteousness, which bind us to Satan's kingdom, will burst and we will inherit the Kingdom of God. For God, nothing is impossible.

37. Self-Will

Only one will can rule, only one will can make the final decision. Either the will of our Creator, the Lord of heaven and earth, which is also revealed to us through the will of our neighbour, or our will. There is no greater example of presumptuousness than when a person, who himself is but a mere creature, seeks to assert his will against the will of his Creator. It is also presumptuousness, when we think that our will, our decisions, our views, our taste are better than those of our fellow men. We are indeed greatly presumptuous, if we insist upon having everything done the way we think it ought to be done. Thus we tell everyone around us that we are the ones to decide everything. Self-will is the expression of great pride, the opposite of humility, which lets us yield our wills to someone else's.

Self-willed people are hard to live with; they ruin community life. On the other hand, people whose wills are at one with God and man are bringers of peace and joy. Self-willed people idolize their own will. They rebel against the will of God and thereby are guilty of witchcraft for "rebellion is as the sin of witchcraft" (1 Sam. 15: 23). We cannot take the sin of self-will seriously enough. Not only does it continually make us sin against our fellow-men, whom we torment when we insist upon having our own way, but it also separates us from God. When we act according to our self-will, we act against the will of God, including the instances where the will of God comes to us through other people.

The Holy Scriptures say that the self-willed are among the cursed children of the last days who will come under God's judgment (2 Pet. 2: 10). That is why we have to get rid of this sin no matter how high the price. There is one small word that will help us fight against this spreading cancer of self-will, which causes so much strife and discord and even ruins many a peaceful fellowship. This one small word is, "Yes"; Yes to the will of God. This word has wonderful power. Jesus said it in Gethsemane, at the time when it probably cost Him more than ever before to surrender His will to the Father's. He overcame the trial with just a few words, "My Father, not as I will but as thou wilt" (Matt. 26: 39). Jesus said Yes to God's will when it was so incomprehensible to Him. Thus He redeemed us to say Yes to the will of God. This we may claim in faith.

Let us keep the picture of Jesus always in our hearts—Jesus, who yielded like a lamb to the will of the Father. Let the beauty of a will completely yielded to God captivate our hearts and let our prayers become serious, "Thy likeness print on me, Jesus, my Master." The Lord will answer our pleas more and more. Jesus not only surrendered to the will of His Father, but He also let Himself be bound to our malicious wills. Thus He can free us from the bonds of our self-will. Because He let Himself be bound, and surrendered His life on the cross, our chains have to be broken. Day by day claim the promises of God in prayer: "He shatters the doors of bronze, and cuts in two the bars of iron" (Ps. 107: 16). If our self-will is also like iron and we think we will never be able to overcome it, we must continue to count upon this fact: When Jesus surrendered His will, He redeemed us so that we can do the same. We must not give up, but keep fighting the battle of faith. It will end in victory.

We should surrender our wills many times a day to God, beginning every morning by expecting God to let things go against our wills during the course of the day. We must ask Him to grant us the grace to say "Yes"—unless someone demands something against our consciences. By voluntarily deciding to obey someone whom we live or work with, we will learn to break our self-will through his instructions. If we give thanks for all the opportunities we have to let our wills be broken through conditions and situations, we shall make the most of them by always humbling ourselves and asking for forgiveness when our first reaction was displeasure or rebellion. If we admit our sin of self-will to people and humble ourselves, our pride will be broken. If we learn how to join the Lamb of God in saying "Yes, Father, I love Your will", our self-will will no longer receive any nourishment, and will starve to death. In this way our wills will be at one with God's will and this unity will bring us deep joy.

The battle against sin is a necessity, because we have an enemy who incites us to sin. The battle of faith, calling upon the name of Jesus and His blood, frees us from the power of this enemy.

Lord Jesus,

Set me free from my self-will, which is enslaving me. Burst the chains of my ego. You have borne these chains for me and surrendered Your will to the Father's when He asked You to suffer. I believe that You have redeemed me and that You have put all self-will under Your feet so that it can no longer reign over me.

In remembrance of how much it cost You to yield Your will in the Garden of Gethsemane, let this be my response: "Not my will, but Thine be done!" Cross my will, over and over again; take away the power and tenacity which it usually uses to assert itself. Let me hear the will of God so that I may be like a downy feather in His hand, which He can blow whither He will, and which He can rule with His will to the glory of Your redemption, which has set me free from bondage to my own will.

38. Slander: Gossip

The Holy Scriptures say that slanderers deserve to die (Rom. 1: 30, 32). Nor should Christians even eat with slanderers (1 Cor. 5: 11—N.E.B.). Paul says: "Drive out the wicked person from among you" (1 Cor. 5: 13). That is how serious the sin of slander is. But Satan is willing to pay any price to get us to sin so that we will be damned one day. He wants us to be not even aware that we have indulged in it; he wants us to think that this sin of slander cannot possibly apply to us! But it is a fact that this sin is very wide-spread among us Christians. It is one of the traits of our Pharisaism. We would not lie intentionally—we are too pious for that—and yet we lie by condemning and accusing others, even if we do not know them personally, but have just heard negative things about them from someone else. Because we are so high and mighty, self-righteous and critical, we think we can do so without testing the facts and so we spread false suppositions. We may begin to spread falsehoods about members of our own church or about other Christian groups without even being aware of it.

In this way the sin of slander creeps unnoticed into our hearts. It begins with the spirit of criticism, with judging one another, with gossiping. In our pride we think we can and must pass judgment on everything, we must assume the job of watchman. But we are wrong. We are not true watchmen, because we have not even watched over the truth in our own lives. And still we dare to condemn others and make statements without having examined the facts. If they are wrong, we become slanderers, who spread false rumours that could ruin the reputation of someone else or of an entire Christian group.

Did the Pharisees do anything different but judge Jesus' actions to the best of their knowledge, and as the spiritual leaders of their people warn others about Him? And yet they were hypocrites, slanderers and liars. How did that come about? Their judgments were not pure. They were not free from personal emotions, even if they did not realize this. They were proud and did not want to be humiliated in front of Jesus, who drew their attention to their sins and their need for redemption. They also had envy in their hearts, because Jesus had many adherents among the people and had placed the Pharisees in the background. That was hard for them to take. They begrudged Him this popularity. That is why judgment about Jesus came from their evil hearts. Such a proud heart, filled with envy and jealousy, makes us blind and incapable of seeing the truth about others. At the same time it gives birth to another sin—gossip, or slander. So it is often the Christians who out of envy, slander their brothers and other Christian groups. They say unfavourable things about others to deprive them of their good reputation, while they want to improve their own reputation as supposed watchmen and good leaders of the church. But they would never admit that they gave such negative verdicts out of envy.

About this attitude Jesus says, "The hour is coming when whoever kills you will think he is offering service to God" (John 16: 2). If we only realized that Satan's most crafty trick is not letting us recognize our lies as lies! In our pride, which makes us blind to our sin of envy, we are convinced that we are serving God, when we warn people about others and so undermine their reputation. No one is in such danger of living in a lie and becoming a hypocrite as we Christians. But because we will all have to appear before the judgment seat of God and answer for everything we have done (2 Cor. 5: 21), we have to closely examine all our judgments about people and Christian groups and ask for light to see where we have fallen into the sin of slander.

Slander belongs to the sin of lying, and liars, according to the Holy Scriptures, will find their place in Satan's kingdom. Besides that, slander belongs to the worst sins against the fifth commandment, because when we destroy a person's good reputation, we can harm him more than if we had wounded him physically. And what a terrible judgment does Jesus threaten to give those who trespass against the fifth commandment, by being angry at their brothers! Again Jesus shows us quite clearly that this sin, if we do not turn from it, will bring us into the kingdom of torment.

So our fate for eternity depends upon whether we are freed from gossip and slander. How angry God must be at slanderers, if He forbids us to eat with them. Never will they have fellowship with other believers in the Kingdom of God—they will be cast out into darkness.

In the face of such severe judgments which await slanderers, it means making a complete "about face" and promising God: "Unless it is necessary, I will not spread any negative stories about others or about Christian groups, and I will never do so without examining them first." Yes, it means entreating Him to grant us contrition about the times when we have done such things, and to turn away from such ways.

Then we have to pray daily: "Set my secret sins in the light of Thy countenance (Ps. 90: 8). Show me my hidden motives for judging others so sharply." Yes, we have to ask God daily to show us the roots of our sins, to show us why we have an aversion for a certain person and can only make unfavourable judgments. Often it is pride, hidden jealousy, envy and bitterness which are the causes. But it is not enough to have this revealed to ourselves, and to confess it to a spiritual counsellor. No, contrition must compel us to go to the others, whom we have put into a bad light through our criticism and slander, and ask them for their forgiveness. Then we have to tell all the others the truth and to set the falsehoods straight.

Repent! That was the contents of Jesus' sermons. Turn away from evil words and actions. If we have slandered others, let that be our motto, so that we will not become an instrument of Satan again. He is the "old liar" who makes every effort to seduce us into slandering. If we do not repent, we will belong to him and he can come for us at the end of our lives and take us into his kingdom of horror.

Jesus wants to help us be freed from the sin of gossip and slander. He has said, "I have come into the world to bear witness to the truth" (John 18: 37). He has redeemed us to be children of light and truth. If He as the Head is truth, would He not make every effort to have the members of His body also bear the traits of truth?

Therefore, "Ask, and it will be given you!" He wants to give us His Spirit of truth; He has promised Him to us, if we ask for Him in faith. He is exhorting us to do this so that He can redeem us from the severe sin of gossip. Through His redemption we will be able to say good things about others in humble love and make every effort to practise the song of love in 1 Corinthians 13.

39. Softness: Laziness

If we are intent upon leading the most comfortable life possible, we are acting contrary to Jesus' command that we should lose our lives and deny ourselves. Jesus says that He only recognizes as His disciples and followers those who follow this command (Luke 14: 26). Yes, if we are lazy and slack, if our longing for comfort and convenience prevents us from doing our work for Jesus well and we do not fight against it, these serious words of Scripture apply to us: "Cursed is he who does the work of the Lord with slackness" (Jer. 48: 10). Do we realize what it means to be cursed by God, whose whole heart yearns to bless? And do we see what judgment slackness and softness will bring us in eternity as well?

If we do not want to come under this curse, whose terrible consequences will be revealed in eternity, we have to renounce all softness, all laziness in our lives; we have to declare war on it. Jesus' cutting words, "Whoever of you does not renounce all that he has cannot be my disciple" (Luke 14: 33) also applies to our work for Jesus. If we cannot give up our demands for comfort, for much free time and rest, for better pay, they will make it impossible for us to use our time and energy for Jesus. If a soldier were laden with many items for his personal comfort, he could never go to war. Nor can we ever become soldiers for Jesus Christ, or true disciples, if we do this. And quite aside from this, softness and laziness open the door to many other sins which really make us unfit for service.

So we have to let Jesus' words pierce our hearts, learn to abhor our softness and love of comfort and in faith renounce what would make us unfit to serve Jesus properly. That means, for instance, giving up our desire for special comforts, for the most beautiful home, for the best interior decorating and for the food that we especially enjoy. Keeping Jesus in mind, whom we want to

follow, we must repent and take a new path, for example
if we have let our family or others serve us more than
necessary, or if we have avoided difficult work and in
these ways have left the path of Jesus. Jesus tells us, "I am
among you as one who serves" (Luke 22: 27). This shows
us Jesus' true glory. Yet the "disciple is not above his
teacher". The sign that we are really disciples of Jesus is
that we renounce our softness, not legalistically, but out
of love for Him. This love will draw us along His way of
denial.

When we serve others, not asking for anything special
or unnecessary, and not expecting any comfort, we are
not only on Jesus' way, we are actually bound to Him.
That is why, in spite of all the sacrifice, it is not a difficult
way. It makes us one with Jesus who is pure love and
tender care and at the same time the almighty Lord.
What should we be afraid of? He cares for us in great
love and fulfils His promise, "He who loses his life"—that
is, who loses whatever he thinks he needs in life—"for my
sake will find it" (Matt. 10: 39). By following Him, we
receive everything we need through His blessing, loving
care and almighty power. Yes, we find that the Father in
heaven cares for His children and gives them an abundance of earthly goods for their nourishment, clothing
and shelter.

Since Jesus left His life, should not we also be able to
leave what makes life worthwhile for us? Scripture says
that He had the power to lay down His life (John 10: 18).
Yes, if we can give up our lives and our demands, we will
have great power and authority.

Jesus wants to give this power to His own. It is the
greatest power; it is greater than the power to work miracles. How do we get it? Through faith! Through faith
the fortresses and strongholds of our hearts will fall, even
the stronghold of wanting to keep our life with all its
demands for comfort.

This battle of faith against softness is more important
than ever before, because we are now approaching "hard
times", times when we will be persecuted for His name's
sake. Now we must conquer all softness and laziness in

the power of Jesus' redemption, so that they will not be our downfall in the hour of temptation. It was not by chance that Peter changed from disciple to betrayer while he was warming himself by the fire.

40. Talkativeness

The Holy Scriptures say time and again that idle talk is a sin, but we usually do not take it seriously. And yet this is a sin that God will judge very severely. It is listed together with immorality and impurity and covetousness, which are not fitting among saints (Eph. 5: 3f). In summary the Apostle Paul says, "Let no one deceive you with empty words, for it is because of these things that the wrath of God comes upon the sons of disobedience. Therefore do not associate with them" (Eph. 5: 6f). Our idle talk incites the wrath of God. And the wrath of God always brings us judgment, if we do not repent. We cannot play around with this sin. Talking is a very serious matter. Our words will not blow away like chaff. They will arise again at the Last Judgment. Not one of them will be lost. One day we must give account of every unprofitable word; we will be judged according to our words (Matt. 12: 36f). And woe, if our tongue, "a restless evil, full of deadly poison" (Jas. 3: 8), was an instrument of evil, because we spoke poisonous, bitter, hate-filled and dirty words.

Since this sin of talkativeness "eats its way like gangrene" (2 Tim. 2: 17), a total operation has to be performed. According to Jesus' words, "If your eye (or tongue) causes you to sin, pluck it out" (Mark 9: 47). Otherwise you will risk being thrown into hell.

What is the way to being set free completely? First we must find the root of talkativeness. Often it is our desire for attention. We want to make ourselves important. We think we have to give our opinion about everything. How quickly these unprofitable words lead us to speak in a disparaging way about others who are not present! Or we begin to gossip and spread rumours, etc. Or sometimes we use idle talk to drown our bad conscience; sometimes we chatter out of laziness, because we do not want to work: sometimes out of bitterness, because we want to let out the poisonous thoughts in us. And there are many more reasons.

The deepest cause of talkativeness is that we are separated from Jesus. A talkative person usually does not speak much with Jesus, for conversation with Jesus makes us quiet and turns our thoughts to God. The less "quiet time" we have, the more talkative we are. Through many empty words and unprofitable talk we lose our liking for the hidden fellowship with Jesus. Everything depends upon giving Jesus more quiet time to listen to Him. When our personal meditation time is over and we return to people, His presence should accompany us and our words should be filled with His Holy Spirit. Then we can no longer tell shady jokes and we will not talk needlessly. We should only say what we would, were Jesus physically in our midst. Then only such talk will come out of our mouths as is good for edifying, as fits the occasion, that it may impart grace to those who hear (Eph. 4: 29).

Certainly it will not be easy for many of us to find time for quiet during the course of a hectic, demanding day. But where there's a will, there's a way. Somehow there will be an opportunity. For instance, we can save time on visits or jobs that are more pleasurable than compulsory and give this time to Jesus. When we leave the quietness of our room and continue to carry on our conversation with Jesus in our hearts, our talking will improve almost by itself. In heaven Jesus will only hold conversations with those who sought Him here in prayer and did not give room to unprofitable talk.

Whoever says, "I do not know what to do with my quiet time" will not get rid of his talkativeness. He does not want to pay anything for the healing of this sinful disease. Patience and practice are required before we can converse with God, that is, before we can pray genuinely. But whoever wants to be freed from talkativeness will take Jesus' promise as a reality, "Behold, I make all things new" (Rev. 21: 5).

Even our tongue will become new, so that it will be an instrument of God's Spirit and can speak His words and will be silent instead of speaking idle talk. Jesus Christ has come to set us free from the slavery of sin, from the evil fire in our tongue that can bring us judgment and hell. He has been given power even over our tongues.

41. Touchiness

If our bodies are sick, they are especially sensitive to cold, draught and other environmental factors. Our souls are sensitive, if our "egos" are sick. Sensitivity or touchiness is the ego's desire for attention. We expect our egos to be spoiled and pampered like a sick body. If that does not happen, if we do not receive love, attention, respect, if we are overlooked or forgotten, if we have been criticized, then we react like a person who is physically sick and make a woeful face. We are hurt, cry and rebel against our neighbours and reproach them. We imagine that people do not have our best interests at heart, that we are not getting what we deserve, that they are being unfair to us. Whenever they say anything, we think they are trying to hurt our reputations. We become unhappy, but at the same time torment and tyrannize those around us through touchiness and egoism. That is why this is not merely an "unfortunate disposition", but a sin which gives birth to many evils, which causes us to heap up guilt upon guilt through our behaviour towards our fellow men. No matter what it costs we have to become free from this sin and begin to wage a campaign against it.

What do touchy people usually do? Instead of declaring war on this sin, they "put their ego to bed", expecting someone to comfort and pamper it. Even if this does happen, it would not get better. For touchiness is an imaginary sickness. Patients with imaginary sicknesses, however, get worse the more they are spoiled. They will only be helped, if people stop making a fuss over them and confront them with the hard reality of life. The same is true for sensitive souls that suffer from the sickness of egoism. They have to be willing to submit to rough treatment.

First of all, we have to accept the diagnosis without making any excuses. It is not the others who are hurting us all the time, but we ourselves, with our egoistic demands for love and respect, are the cause of our troubles. We are the guilty ones when there are tensions. They can only be solved if we repent of our sin of egoism, which is a sin against love. For Jesus has redeemed us so that we will live no longer for ourselves, for our ego, but for Him who died for our sake (2 Cor. 5: 15), and also live for our fellow men. Egoists are always hurt easily. They destroy every harmonious situation and make the redemption of Jesus unbelievable, giving offence to others who are just beginning to follow Jesus. So without our realizing it, our egoism can make others stop believing in Jesus and thus expose them to the greatest danger. How terrible it will be on the judgment day when their accusations will pass judgment upon us.

We have to make every possible effort to get rid of our egoism. The word shows that we are slaves of our egos. Our thinking centres around our ego instead of around Jesus, and yet we have been called to have Him as the Centre of our lives. But if the most important thing in our life is satisfying our egos with attention, love, respect and other good things, we can never enter Jesus' kingdom above. There everything centres around Jesus, free from every selfish bond. Our touchiness has to be overcome, and it can be overcome, because Jesus has come to free us from our sins.

What is the way? Not to pay any attention to oneself, not to make any more demands for love, attention, respect. This has to be done in a practical way. We must make a commitment to God—a written one—believing in His redemption. Let us say to the Lord,

> In future I no longer want to receive any attention; I don't want to try to get love and respect and understanding; I want to accept criticism and reproach. I want my ego and its demands to starve to death so that I can have room in my heart for You, Jesus, and Your love which did not seek itself, but let its own demands die and only sought others. Let me tread Your path and bring fruit for You. I believe in

Your words: "Whoever would save his life will lose it, and whoever loses his life for my sake will find it" (Matt. 16: 25).

Yes, I want to be freed from this sin quickly. So I will strive in faith to be able to say, "Thank You God", for every rough treatment. You have given me what I have asked for. By chastening my ego, You want to help me be freed from my touchiness. In thanksgiving I take the redemption from my touchiness, which you have gained for me. In spirit I behold the new man, released and joyful, and no longer clouded by touchiness.

But because the road is long, we must not get tired or discouraged when we continually fall down. We have to endure to the end, in faith that Jesus' redemption has set us free, until we can see what we have believed. Could anything be impossible for God? Jesus' blood cleanses us from all sin, no matter how strong and persistent it might be. He is greater than everything else, even greater than the uncanny power of our egos. Still it is necessary to endure in faith and not to get tired. We must spend a long time calling upon the victorious name JESUS and praising its power over our sin. If Jesus calls Himself the Redeemer, He will not let His name be put to shame, but will put His honour at stake and prove that He can really break this bondage to sin.

It is meaningless only to call upon the name Jesus and His victory without being willing to place ourselves in God's hands and let Him chasten us because of sinful traits. This chastening will cleanse us. Only if we do both, will we reach the goal.

42. Unlovingness

The greatest thing of all—in time and in eternity—is love. That is why there is no greater guilt than the sin against love. We were created in the image of God, who is Love, and after the fall we were redeemed to love through our Lord Jesus Christ. Nothing pierces God's heart more deeply than our not reflecting His image of love. Yes, the Apostle Paul states in 1 Corinthians 13 that we are nothing and that our supposedly loving deeds like "giving away all we have" or "delivering our bodies to be burned" are also nothing. All our words and actions, our whole being, have to be filled with love; otherwise, no matter what we do, we will constantly become guilty towards others.

What does unlovingness include? It is passing by one's neighbour's needs and gentle requests; it is the beginning of unmercifulness. We are not really interested in others; we are not merciful to them; we do not sympathize with them. We cannot rejoice with our neighbours and we cannot cry with them. We do not spoil them with our love, we are not kind to them when they are overlooked or humiliated. Sometimes our forgetfulness, which we try to excuse by saying that we had so much to do, is nothing but our great unwillingness to love others. But even when we seem to be working for others and busily helping them, we may actually only be trying to satisfy our own egos. Then we do not hear the Holy Spirit, when He quietly admonishes us; and when it is really important, when others really need our help, we can be very unloving.

There are not enough words to express all the damage unlovingness can do. Without realizing it, we can drive sad and discouraged people into despair, we can crush their souls by taking away their last hope. And yet we think that we have not done anything wicked, we were "just a bit unloving". But if we try to make this sin of unlovingness seem harmless, we are deceiving ourselves. We have not seen our behaviour in Jesus' light and heard what He has to, say about it. That is the only thing that matters and we will be judged accordingly one day. One of the most amazing words of judgment that Jesus spoke, that hits us to the core, was directed at the unloving, who pass by the needs of others, "Depart from me, you cursed!" (Matt. 25: 41). Only if we have been "shaken up" by these words, will we no longer be able to persevere blindly in the sin of unlovingness.

Because it is so easy for us to deceive ourselves through self-righteousness, we ought to yearn to see our words and actions towards our neighbours in the light of God. He has to show us our unlovingness so that we will fight against it. At the end of our life we will be judged according to love. Then it will be of no avail to prove that we have not committed any coarse sins such as betrayal, blasphemy or slander. For the Holy Scriptures include this sin of unlovingness in its list of serious sins (Rom. 1: 31; 2 Tim. 3: 3). And when Jesus pronounces His devastating verdict, "Depart from me, you cursed", it means "into the eternal fire prepared for the devil and his angels" (Matt. 25: 41).

Whoever does not want God to pass this sentence on him has to get to the bottom of his unlovingness in order to deal with it. The root of unlovingness is self-love. We love ourselves so much, and are so involved in ourselves, that we do not have any interest or time left over for others. Why do we love ourselves so much? Because we are separated from God, the eternal Love. "By this we know we love the children of God, when we *love God*" (1 John 5: 2). We do not love God; that is the real reason for our sin of unlovingness.

That is the first thing that we must recognize: our relationship to God is not in order. We have not given Him our first love; we are not at one with Him. That is why love cannot stream forth from our hearts to others. Instead we are indifferent, or what is even worse, harsh to everyone or to certain people. We are living apart from Jesus, ignoring His commandment to love others.

This is where we have to begin to repent. We must ask for a repentant heart, because we do not love God and our neighbour. God, who has promised to answer earnest prayer, will let us repent of our sin against the first commandment, not loving God above all things and our neighbour as ourselves. If we come to Jesus' cross with a repentant heart, we will hear His words, "It is finished!", "Fear not, for I have redeemed you!" He has also redeemed us from our unlovingness so that we can love. Yes, these words, "It is finished", have opened a new fount; His love will flow into us through His precious blood.

Love has been purchased for us. Whoever asks for it will receive it. He will receive eyes to see the needs and sufferings of others, hands which do good deeds, and above all a heart that is on fire and overflows with love. Could there be any other prayer which Jesus would rather answer than the prayer for love? Scripture says that it is the greatest of all. He has redeemed us so that we may be remade in His image, so that we may bear the image of love, the most beautiful image that man can bear. By loving, we will learn how to love. Then we will receive grace at the end of our life, when we have to appear before the judgment seat of Christ. Instead of hearing the devastating words, "Depart from me, you cursed", we will hear the words of grace, "Come, O blessed of my Father. inherit the kingdom!" (Matt. 25: 34).

O Jesus, since You are perfect Love, I will ask You: Do not tolerate anything in me that goes against love. Help me to hate my unlovingness and grant me a repentant heart, which will lead to new life.

Grant me eyes to see when I have passed by others, when I have hurt them. Give me Your light and show me when I have let others wait in vain for a loving glance, word or deed. Because You have shed Your blood to redeem me to love, You must see Your redemption manifest in my life. I will not give up, until this change comes to pass in me, that Your love comes to life in me and flows forth from me. To the glory of Your name You will accomplish this and lead me to eternal salvation in Your kingdom.

AMEN.

43. Unreliability

An unreliable person is one who says: "Yes, yes" and then does not do it, just like the first son of the parable of the father and the two sons. Jesus preferred the second son although he said "No" at first (Matt. 21: 28–31). The unreliable, even when they do not promise to do anything, are always irresponsible. They let God and people wait. They disappoint them by not doing what they are told to do and are not very concerned about the trouble they have caused. Such irresponsible attitudes can often form a chain of difficulties at work and can cause great loss of goods or money.

Irresponsible people cost their fellow men much time and energy and make life difficult for them.

They are not interested in how much trouble they cause others. Yet with this attitude they sin against love and this is a serious sin. It separates us from God and His love (1 John 4: 8), here on earth and even more so in eternity, where the irresponsible, who thought this personality trait was harmless and perhaps excused it by saying it was due to their congeniality, will be greatly astonished. Because this sin will have serious consequences in eternity, the first thing we have to do is to break with it and not to try to justify it. As long as we justify ourselves, we can be sure that Satan is holding us tight in his claws. Then this sin will have piled up a mountain of guilt against us on the day of judgment. So we have to take seriously this sin, which we often think is harmless, and fight against it to the point of shedding blood. For behind the sin of unreliability there are other sins like self-will, indifference and superficiality. Or we are so involved in our own affairs that we avoid the inconvenience of carrying out something reliably for someone else.

But the deepest fault of the unreliable is that they do not live in the sight of God. They usually make their first mistake by not taking an obligation, a promise, or a commission seriously. They only listen with one ear, because they do not do their work for God and in His presence. They are not particularly interested in doing their work as well as possible in order to please Jesus. But whether we work for weeks, months or years for a certain project, it will all be in vain, and will one day be thrown into the fire of judgment, if we do not do it with God.

If we do not want to find that all our activities are in vain and do not want to come under God's judgment, we have to begin to listen carefully when people tell us things, as though we were hearing a message directly from God, which is a matter of life and death, so that we do not miss a single word. If we tend to forget easily, we should begin to take requests, admonitions and orders seriously, by taking notes. We must do so in the knowledge that we are then taking God seriously, who has given us this task and is seeking a faithful steward. We must immediately do what we are told and not put anything off. Every time we carry out a task, we should call upon God to give us the grace to do everything properly. In faith we must ask the Lord to stand before our eyes so that we can do everything for Him and not for other people. Let this sin serve to make us strive to lead a life in the presence of God. Jesus has redeemed us for this.

It is written that Jesus was found "faithful in God's house" (Heb. 3: 2). And He has ransomed us to bear His image. Especially in our times when so many will not believe the *words* of the Gospel, as members of His body we should *live* a credible witness in the world by being faithful and reliable even in the smallest things. Through Jesus' sacrifice we are freed from the power of unreliability. Therefore, we will be freed, if we continually ask Him to fulfil the promise that He gave us in His Word. "He condemned sin in the flesh" (Rom. 8: 3) so that sin can no longer rule over us, and our members might become instruments of His grace.

44. Worldly Love: Bondage to People and Things of this Earth

When the Apostle Paul wrote, "Demas, in love with this present world" (2 Tim. 4: 10), he meant that Demas had forsaken him and the work of Jesus Christ; he had fallen away. For "if anyone loves the world, love for the Father is not in him" (1 John 2: 15); he is under someone else's dominion, under the "prince of this world" and loves his sphere of influence. We often think that "worldly love" is harmless and we try to justify it with such camouflage as, "I am just open to the world and not narrow-minded". Yet worldly love is a dangerous sin; it brings us into the hands of Jesus' enemy.

In order not to fall into such self-deception, we have to discern whether we love the world as "God so loved the world" (John 3: 16) or as the prince of this world tries to make us love it. An example of having the right relationship to the world is the Apostle Paul. He also lived in the world and used its gifts and goods and rejoiced in them, *but* giving thanks to God. In everything he loved and honoured the Creator of all gifts and praised Him for them. His joy in everything that was created was his joy in God who bestowed the gifts upon him. That is why it did not matter whether he had worldly goods or not; he was completely free from them. He could only rejoice in them when God gave them to him.

But it is dreadful if we should live for the world instead of for God, that is, if we should love the people, goods and possessions of this world apart from God and be bound to them.

Then these words apply to us: We can only serve God *or* mammon, i.e. the world; we can only love God *or* the world. To love means to be completely committed to that which we love. For whatever we are completely committed to takes over God's place in our lives. Therefore, worldly love is idol worship, a serious sin, which will bring us the judgment of God. For could there be any greater sin than having an idol when the first commandment in Scripture is to love God above all things? In Revelation 21: 8 it says that idolaters will be sentenced to the lake that burns with fire and brimstone. That is what the Apostle John writes to a Christian Church about idolatry, not the idolatry of the Old Testament but rather the idols of their profession, family, reputation, art, nature, or anything that is a gift from God.

Because worldly love binds us to the prince of this world, who wants to bring us into his kingdom of darkness, we have to make a definite decision not to choose the world, but to choose Jesus as our great love and the centre of our lives. The Apostle Paul shows how when he writes, "Let those who have wives live as though they had none ... and those who buy as though they had no goods, and those who deal with the world as though they had no dealing with it" (1 Cor. 7: 29–31). That is, in every relationship to people or things of the world, Jesus must be the centre; our thoughts and emotions must centre around Him. Then we will love other people and things only through Christ. So we can either have things or not have them. The centre, Jesus, will remain. "All are yours; and you are Christ's" (1 Cor. 3: 22, 23) and the last part is the important one.

But if worldly love has taken a hold of us in any form, this sin will separate us from God even here on earth. There is not much difference whether we are bound to the things of this world which in and of themselves are good, like art, science and nature, or to people, who have been created by God—or whether we are directly bound to a sinful lust. Bondage is bondage! It prevents us from being available for God; it chains us to Satan, the prince of this world. For only those who are free for God will be bound by Jesus in love. He is only interested in our love. And since He is the only One who can give us love as no man can, He can also make such an absolute demand upon us. He can demand that we radically turn away from every bondage and love, which takes love away from Him. He also says this about our families, about our parents, whom we are supposed to love and honour; if we love them more than we love Jesus, we are not worthy of Him and we lose the right to be called His disciples (Matt. 10: 37).

Jesus confronts us with this question: "What and whom do you love?" He does not say, "My own should no longer have families, they should not be interested in art and science or other similar things." He is only concerned about love—about what has the first place in our hearts, what our hearts are most attached to. But then He demands a radical break. He expects us to leave people and goods that we are attached to in a false manner, out of love for Him. He calls to us: "Every one who has left houses or brothers or sisters or father or mother or children or lands, for my name's sake . . ." (Matt. 19: 29).

Yes, Jesus does not only go so far as saying that we should not love father or mother *more* than Him, but He also demands, "If any one comes to me and does not hate his own father and mother, he cannot be my disciple" (Luke 14: 26). That applies to the situation when parents want to prevent us from placing our lives at Jesus' disposal. We should hate our sinful egos and everyone who wants to convince us to live for these egos and other things in this world. Hatred is the opposite of toleration. Jesus demands that we no longer tolerate our relationships with people whom we love in a false manner so that our heart and our thoughts are completely captivated by them. This is what He means by hating and forsaking.

That means more than making a clear decision. If, for instance, we are bound to a person, to break free might involve burning his letters and pictures. Or if love for art has captivated us, we ought to give away our art collection. Or if a high standard of living is our idol, we must get rid of our luxuries and reset our standards according to the Gospel. If the "television idol" rules over us, we must break away from the T.V. set.

Whatever we hate we can no longer tolerate, we have to destroy it somehow. We must declare war on this sin of worldly love, if we do not want our life to become powerless and we do not want to fall into the hands of the enemy. Jesus hates sin as much as He loves sinners, and He demands that His own also hate sin.

But how can we become free from our bondage? Only love for Jesus can help us. If we really love Jesus, we will let go of all of the things almost automatically. But what should we do, if we do not love Jesus enough and people and things still have so much power over us? First we must ask for a repentant heart for our worshipping idols and insulting God. In addition we must constantly praise the power of the blood of the Lamb over our bondages. It has power to break chains. It was shed to bring release.

Jesus is asking us, "Are you willing to be freed from the sin of worldly love?" His blood will only be effective for those who really *want* to be freed. We can believe that Jesus will grant us the earnest will to be free, if we do not yet have it, for He has also died and arose from the dead for the sake of our unwillingness. He wants to free us from this worldly love, because he knows that it binds us to the prince of this world, Satan, and a terrible fate will await us after death. We will be slaves in Satan's kingdom. But Jesus wants to grant us joy for time and eternity, free from chains to darkness. That is why He exhorts us, "Do not love the world or the things in the world . . . the lust of the flesh and the lust of the eyes and the pride of life. The world passes away, and the lust of it; but he who does the will of God abides for ever" (1 John 2: 15–17) with Jesus in His kingdom.

45. Worrying

Worrying is a problem that most people have. Worries come when we think about the future. Let us consider an example. If a father becomes sick and has not yet provided for his children, worry begins to take hold of him. What will happen to the children, if the illness gets worse? Who will take care of them? Or there are threats of war or riots. Or there might be monetary inflation. Then we begin to worry about whether our savings will decrease in value, whether we will have a steady income, or whether we will lose our security.

Or we begin to worry about our children and how they are growing up, especially if they begin to do things of which we do not approve. Or worries may arise due to marital problems. Whether it be in physical or spiritual matters, in public or personal matters—the more variety modern man seems to have, the more variety his worries have.

Because our well-being, and the well-being of our families, is never completely secure for the future, we are never secure from attacks of worry. Usually we feel sorry for ourselves, because we think we have so many things to worry about and they irritate us.

But Jesus says something different about worrying. Jesus says that worrying is the business of the heathen. Worrying grows out of an unchristian attitude (Matt. 6: 32). Therefore, worrying is a sin. Why? Worrying means that our hearts are not rooted in the Kingdom of God and we do not seek it above all; we do not have God in the centre of our lives. We do not seek the Kingdom of God, because we are not captivated by it. Rather we are captivated by things that are more important to us; a steady income, good health, recognition, well-being of body and soul for ourselves and our families. These are the centre of our thoughts.

But this cannot stay that way. For then God will say

that we belong to the heathen, who do not know a living God, and are not His own, His children. If we are influenced by the spirit of worrying, the reason lies in our disbelief, in our discouragement. We worry, because we do not believe that God as a Father will take care of us. But when Scripture tells us about the cowardly and the faithless, it says, "their lot shall be in the lake that burns with fire and brimstone, which is the second death" (Rev. 21: 8). So at all costs we have to overcome our spirit of worry so that the enemy will not have a right to claim us. Not only for the sake of eternity, but also for the sake of our peace of mind here, we have to be freed. It is not the actual needs and sufferings, but rather worrying that brings sorrow into our lives. That is why we have to get to the bottom of this matter and find out what is the root of our worrying in order to ask how we can overcome it.

The root of worrying is our fear of the cross. Worrying is nourished by the fear that we can lose some of the benefits we possess for body or soul, security or comfort. Then we would have to suffer—and we cannot commit ourselves to this suffering. We want to protect ourselves from the difficult things that lie ahead of us. So our worrying thoughts centre around how we can avoid the difficulties.

In our pride we often think we can master our lives alone, independent of God's help. When we come to the end of our possibilities, our worries, nourished by our fear of suffering, begin to captivate us.

Therefore, the way to begin to overcome this sin of worrying is to commit ourselves to suffering! We must say "Yes" to all the difficult things that are in our hearts. In spirit, we must lay upon the altar of sacrifice everything that we want to hold on to at any cost and say:

> *Take my life and everything that makes life worthwhile and precious for me, my health, my dear ones, my security, my wishes and whatever else I have and would like to keep for the future! I surrender my will to You, if You want to take every-*

thing from me. I will not cling to anything any more, because I trust You, my God and my Father, and You will take care of me and my family and give us everything we need in the future. I will only expect help from You. You will not disappoint me. Up until now You have always sustained me, and because You are always the same, You will also sustain me in difficult times.

If we picture in our minds who our Father is, and declare His wonderful traits, then every worry must yield in the sight of His omnipotence and love. Every time we commit ourselves to suffering, let us say to Him:

God, You are my Father, who has lovingly thought of all that I, Your child, need. I trust that You will give me everything I need, especially in times of trouble. You will take care of me. My Father, You will sustain me. You will not let me be tempted beyond my strength. As a Father, You have prepared a way for me and my family. I trust You! My Father, You are greater than all troubles which could possibly come upon me! Your power is stronger and You will help me!

It is absolutely necessary to arrive at this "Yes, Father" prayer, if we want to be freed from the spirit of worrying. Otherwise it will bring us into misfortune and our "heathen" worries will really materialize. We can see this when we look at the people of Israel in the desert. They are filled with worries that the future would be dreadful and that they would perish in the desert. And then the Lord said, Yes, exactly what Israel declared in its mistrust and worrying spirit would come to pass—and they did perish in the desert (Num. 14: 28ff). But those who trusted God and said that He would sustain them, found that He did sustain them. They did not die in the desert and they could take over the promised land.

Whatever we expect from God will happen! If we are

full of worries, we do not expect anything good from God. That is why we will not experience the good things that God has actually planned for us. We are destroying them through our worrying. Worrying is the opposite of trusting the Father. Worrying has to do with unbelief, which has to be overcome at all costs, because it really excludes us from the "promised land" which contains all physical and spiritual wealth and blessings for us.

If it is hard for us to trust in faith, we should begin, as I mentioned, by describing who the Father is and how He will help. And the spirit of worry will be silenced. For the spirit of trust is more powerful than the spirit of worry, which comes from the devil. We must cling to the promise in His word, "Cast all your anxieties upon him, for he cares about you" (1 Peter 5: 7). We should then make a prayer out of all our worries by bringing them to our Father, according to the Apostle Paul's exhortation, "Have no anxiety about anything, but in everything by prayer and supplication with thanksgiving let your requests be made known to God." Then we will find "the peace of God, which passes all understanding" (Phil. 4: 6, 7).

But then follows the second piece of advice that Jesus gives us for the battle against the sin of worry; "But seek first his kingdom ..." (Matt. 6: 33). In the present time, which God has granted as a time of grace, we must live completely for His Kingdom. We must spend ourselves, all our time and energy for His work. We must invest time in prayer and money in His work. If we do this we shall begin to discover what the Lord's promise really means. Now and in the future, whenever trouble may knock on our door, our Father will keep His word, "... all these things shall be yours as well" (Matt. 6: 33).

Whoever takes care of Jesus' work and sacrifices time, money and energy for it, will find that the Lord will take care of him. In times of trouble he will experience the miracles and tender loving care of the Father, he will be sustained and receive help for body, soul and spirit in wonderful ways. His Word is Yea and Amen. Therefore, we must act according to His Word and we will receive help. The spirit of worry must yield when we call upon the name of God the Father and our Lord Jesus Christ. In this way we will set up a signpost declaring the omnipotence and goodness of God. His Name will be glorified through people who are comforted and secure, because all their worries have been quieted in Him.

Other Books by Basilea Schlink
Which You May Wish to Read:

I Found the Key to the Heart of God
The intriguing autobiography of Basilea Schlink.
Original title: *Er Zeigt Der Wege Sinn*, 1968. Foreign translations: 16

My All for Him
A moving collection of powerful meditations on the demands of God upon Christians, and the happiness which follows obedience.
Original title: *Alles Fuer Einen*, 1969. Foreign translations: 12

You Will Never Be the Same
A highly illuminating series of short chapters describing how to successfully deal with specific sins still clinging to the Christian's life.
Original title: *So Wird Man Anders*, 1971. Foreign translations: 17

Ruled by the Spirit
The power of God available today to dedicated Christians. Plus testimonies from among the Sisterhood which indicate how an invigorating working relationship with the Holy Spirit may be enjoyed.
Original title: *Wo Der Geist Weht*, 1967. Foreign translations: 11

Father of Comfort
Short devotions for each day of the year, intended to teach how to trust God as Father.
Original title: *Der Niemand Traurig Sehen Kann*, 1965. Foreign translations: 14

Hidden in His Hands
Devotional readings written to help you prepare for the uncertain future.
Foreign translations: 6

Behold His Love
This book is addressed to those who desire to meditate prayerfully on the passion of Jesus, so that they may be led more and more into the way of the cross and into the unity of love with those who love Him.

A Matter of Life and Death
The rape of planet earth—what caused it, and what to do to remedy it. Carefully documented treatment of the widely discussed problem of global pollution.
Original title: *Umweltverschmutzung Und Dennoch Hoffnung*, 1972. Foreign translations: 6

World in Revolt (booklet)
An astute review and analysis of the waves of revolution rolling over the modern world, and a plain statement on what can be done about it.

Praying Our Way Through Life (booklet)
Counsel on how to react to God during suffering, times of unanswered prayer, temptations, worry, despondency, and fear.
Original title: *Mein Beten*, 1969. Foreign translations: 15

Mirror of Conscience (booklet)
A guidebook to earnest Christians genuinely interested in examining the areas of their lives in which they need victory.
Foreign translations: 16